A PLACE OF EXILE

The European Settlement of New South Wales

A PLACE OF EXILE

The European Settlement
of New South Wales

David Mackay

Melbourne
OXFORD UNIVERSITY PRESS
Auckland NewYork Oxford

OXFORD UNIVERSITY PRESS

Oxford New York Toronto
Delhi Bombay Calcutta Madras Karachi
Kuala Lumpur Singapore Hong Kong Tokyo
Nairobi Dar es Salaam Cape Town
Melbourne Auckland
and associates in
Beirut Berlin Ibadan Mexico City Nicosia

National Library of Australia
Cataloguing-in-Publication data:

Mackay, David, 1944–
A place of exile.

Bibliography.
Includes index.
ISBN 0 19 554632 6.

1. Penal colonies, British. 2. Australia — History — To 1788.
3. Great Britain — Politics and government — 1760–1789. I. Title.

994.01

Typeset by Computype Export, Wellington, New Zealand
Printed in Hong Kong
Published by Oxford University Press, 7 Bowen Crescent, Melbourne
OXFORD is a trademark of Oxford University Press

CONTENTS

To Frances
who brings me luck

ABBREVIATIONS

Add. MSS	British Library, Additional Manuscripts
B.M. (N.H.) D.T.C.	British Museum (Natural History), Banks MSS
H.M.C.	Historical Manuscripts Commission
H.R.A.	Historical Records of Australia
H.R.N.S.W.	Historical Records of New South Wales
I.O.	India Office Library
Kew B.C.	Kew Gardens Herbarium Library, Banks MSS
M.L.	Mitchell Library, State Library of New South Wales
N.L.	National Library of Australia, Canberra
N.L.S.	National Library of Scotland
P.R.O.	Public Record Office
ADM	Admiralty Records
B.T.	Board of Trade Records
C.O.	Colonial Office Records
H.O.	Home Office Records
T.	Treasury Records
S.R.O.	Scottish Record Office

PREFACE

In at least one sense this book can be viewed as an example of that most delicate art — the eating of humble pie. In an article published in 1981 about the neglected imperial outpost at Botany Bay, I was rather flippant at the expense of those involved in the debate about the origins of the convict settlement in New South Wales. The article suggested that the debate had outrun its logistical support in terms of documentation, and it therefore stated the writer's intention of avoiding further embroilment. In this book I apply to rejoin the argument and to re-examine that logistical support.

This *volte face* had its origins in a symposium on the foundation of Australia, held at King's College, London, in May 1982. On that occasion I found myself in sharp opposition to an argument which sought an explanation for the choice of Botany Bay in terms of a coherent and imaginative imperial policy. In my preparation for the symposium I became convinced that this interpretation was incorrect and of the existence of evidence to support an alternative view. The lively interest at the gathering encouraged me to believe that the debate was still very much alive, and likely to intensify as the bicentenary of the sailing of the first fleet approached.

I am grateful to those people who have provided support of various kinds during the period over which I developed my thesis. Professor Glyndwr Williams of Queen Mary College and Professor Peter Marshall of King's College, London, organized the symposium in 1982 and generously entertained its participants. A number of friends and colleagues have read and commented on drafts of the book, particularly Peter McPhee and Ian Macduff of Victoria University of Wellington. Alan Frost, with views very different from my own, has always contributed to the amicable and healthy spirit of the debate. When my research time in London was running out in 1982, John Balow generously assisted me in gathering material, and took a lively interest in where it was all leading.

The staff of the following libraries and record offices provided generous assistance: in London, the British Library, Public Record Office, Royal Botanic Gardens, Kew, the India Office Library, the

British Museum (Natural History), and the Institute of Historical Research; in Scotland, the National Library of Scotland and the Scottish Record Office; in Australia, the State Library of New South Wales and the National Library.

In the production phases of the book I received vital help from Colin Boswell and Annette Garcia who introduced me to the intricacies of document preparation on the IBM 4341. In Melbourne Hilary McPhee provided useful and encouraging professional advice.

I am grateful to the Council of the Victoria University of Wellington for the provision of research leave and funding, and to my colleagues in the History Department for their advice and encouragement.

I would like to thank Dale Farrar for her support during the ups and downs of writing and producing the book.

David Mackay
Wellington, August 1984

Chapter 1

INTRODUCTION

In September 1786 the distinguished surgeon, Sir Charles Blagden, wrote to Sir Joseph Banks about some recent London news: 'The scheme of sending the convicts to New Holland is I think generally disapproved, very much from the apprehension of their being a nest of pirates'.[1] Although this opinion would not have been welcome to Banks, who after all supported the plan, it was certainly widely shared in England at the time and upheld by some elements of the London press. The geographer Alexander Dalrymple had expressed similar fears, particularly because of his interest in the East India Company trade.[2]

These rather gloomy predictions were incorrect. Access to all kinds of boats was strictly controlled in the early years of the colony and when there was an occasional escape by sea, the culprits were soon rounded up and returned to Sydney. Far from increasing or perpetuating criminal activity, Botany Bay eventually had the opposite effect; filtering out the 'convict stain' from its miscreant early colonists. The expectations of Botany Bay which Blagden was reporting were out of step with reality.

Not all forecasts for the convict colony were so gloomy and a small number of men, such as Governor Arthur Phillip and Sir Joseph Banks, foresaw a bright imperial future for New South Wales. Phillip imagined himself in a more flattering situation than the governor of mere convicts, and Banks too wished to lend his name to an enterprise with a more elevated purpose. The other supporters of the settlement ranged from unemployed seamen to undersecretaries of state, and they had their own expectations based on Utopian vision, self interest or official position. The question of expectations has also come to play a critical role in the debate about the origins of the penal colony in New South Wales. The speculative proposals of private individuals have been superimposed on the official documents to produce a distorted but more edifying explanation for the choice of Botany Bay.

The particular predicament of the ministry of William Pitt between 1784 and 1787 has been the element which has perpetuated this confusion. Having publicly declared their attachment to economy, the ministers had the difficult task of justifying what was at the time a ludicrously expensive solution to the convict problem. For the young Prime Minister, committed to the principles of Lord North's Commission for Examining the Public Accounts, sending convicts to New South Wales was a potentially embarrassing decision, and one which required careful manoeuvring.

As if the ministry's own credentials and credibility were not problematic enough, in June 1785 the House of Commons Committee on Transportation narrowed the room for manoeuvre by recognizing the potential costs of transportation to a much more accessible site, and stating the need for some compensating advantages. It expressed a concern that government should 'fix on such Spots for the transportation of Criminals as may by the Commercial and Political Advantages to be derived from them indemnify the Public for the Original charge'.[3] Such a prescription was difficult enough to meet for the proposed site at Das Voltas Bay in present-day Namibia: it was all but impossible for New South Wales.

As information became available about the alarming costs of transporting convicts to so distant and isolated a spot, Pitt and his ministers were obliged to bluster and dissemble about the supposed advantages of such an improbable choice. All but the best-informed and persistent eighteenth-century critics were deceived. Many twentieth-century historians have been similarly persuaded. They have rejected the view that the dumping of convicts was the government's chief priority and have looked for more positive reasons for the choice of Botany Bay. The most recent and compelling expression of this approach is in Alan Frost's study, *Convicts and Empire. A Naval Question.*

At the risk of treading on much traversed ground, it is necessary to outline this thesis and locate it in its proper historiographical context. Frost argued that in response to a French threat to Britain's Indian empire:

Pitt and his advisers decided, quite deliberately, to use the convicts to build a new base that would increase the nation's capacity to protect her Eastern establishment. After considering sites about the southern coasts of Africa, they selected Botany Bay instead.

and again:

Historians have for long considered that the Pitt administration decided to colonize Botany Bay suddenly and in some despair, with the sole aim of ridding the nation's prison [sic] and hulks of the too-numerous transportees. The very opposite is, in fact, true—Pitt and his colleagues took this decision after an extensive and careful consideration; and their broad motive for it was the same as that for their earlier interest in Das Voltas Bay: Botany Bay was a place where they might use the convicts' labour to increase the nation's capacity to protect her position and commerce in the East.[4]

In this view of the origins of New South Wales, the convict problem in England is pushed aside as the primary motive for annexation, and precedence is given to broader strategic and imperial needs.

The persistence of this explanation in modern scholarship cannot be accounted for solely in terms of differing interpretations of the evidence. There are strong arguments for seeing it as the logical development of a tradition of historical scholarship which has the capacity to distort our understanding of Australia's past. It is perhaps ironic that in an age when great distinction is attached to an ability to trace one's antecedents back to the convicts of the first fleet, a group of historians appear determined to underplay the role of convicts in the origins of New South Wales. In place of the traditional explanation, a more exalted account has been constructed, which fits the foundation of the penal colony into the context of a wider imperial purpose.

This process was begun by K.M. Dallas when he described a 'mercantilist spirit' which made Botany Bay an integral part of Britain's growing sea power. This gave birth to the idea that the achievements of the great would offset the failings of the many:

In spite of these 'birth stains' we have become a credit to the Empire through the genius of Macarthur, Marsden, Macquarie, Wentworth and their heirs and successors, helped of course by the heroic explorers and gold prospectors.

Michael Roe also believed that 'the convicts were but tools of broader historical forces', and the foundation of Australia was part of England's 'new imperialism', and in keeping with the 'temper of the age'. This notion of some sort of pervading ethos was echoed by one reviewer of Frost's book, who claimed that its conclusions were 'in accord with the geopolitical facts and the spirit of the age'. In an epilogue to his book, Frost himself referred to his 'search for a less gratuitous beginning for Australia'. Earlier he derided the interpretation which portrayed 'the rag and bone shop of Australia's beginning . . .'. [5]

The general sense is that Australia's colonial past is tawdry and requires tidying up. In their search for more noble and 'rational' explanations for the British annexation of New South Wales, the writers have attempted to erase a blot from Australia's history and to create a new legend of national origin. Once the broader historical forces behind the Botany Bay decision are thus delineated, convicts become mere accessories to the greater endeavour. The argument has parallels in those efforts to portray the early convict population as the almost innocent, and certainly repressed, victims of a pernicious and aristocratic system of government. [6]

Those who have discovered strategic or commercial explanations of white Australia's origins are embracing a Whig view of history. In such an interpretation the foundation of New South Wales becomes an aspect of Britain's stately emergence as a world power. The reasons for this emergence are seen as both economic and political. The liberating force of economic individualism produced an expansion of commerce in the second half of the eighteenth century. Free from the economic constraints of a corporate society, creative energies were diverted into industrial and commercial enterprise. In its eagerness to assist traders, government developed a coherent and expansionist imperial policy which was supported by a powerful navy. The great eighteenth-century voyages of exploration opened up new regions for development, and with solid government backing, merchants rushed in to exploit the new opportunities.

In the constitutional and political realm, the Whig interpretation traces through the emergence of free and democratic societies, untrammelled by feudal restrictions or despotic powers. The key features in this development were the organic growth of representative institutions, the creation of an impartial and independent judiciary, and a system of checks and balances regulating the interaction of the different parts of the constitution. The noble and lasting achievement of this period was the emergence of a sovereign Parliament. The end good to result from this liberation of economic forces and political institutions was progress and prosperity.

From this viewpoint, the original explanation for the foundation of New South Wales can be seen as an affront to Whig values. A guarded penal colony, run along military lines, without representative institutions, and designed to have a subsistence economy, confounds the impulse to progress and prosperity. This would represent a squandering of economic opportunities, a restraint on trade, and a return to tyranny. The tendency of many historians has therefore been to emphasize Australia's march towards prosperity, and to suppress the 'gratuitous' elements in her history. But as Michael Roe has himself observed, such an emphasis on progress leads to elements of the past being underplayed: 'The Whigs give relatively little attention to aborigines or convicts, tending to present them as marginal or picturesque.'[7] The central focus too often has been upon economic developments and their consequences; studies of the rural frontier have until recently taken precedence over urban changes. Issues such as land struggles, the rise of the labour movement, and the emergence of nationalism have occupied the centre of the historical stage.

In terms of historical synthesis, this tradition has had difficulty incorporating the first thirty years of the European presence in Australia, and has tended to rush through what is frequently regarded as rather unsafe territory. Because of these problems the historiography of the period has a particular configuration. There is a heavy weighting towards biography—itself often a Whiggish art—and towards some excellent but close narrative and documentary studies, such as those of Cobley. But there is a suggestion too, that many of the topics for study before 1820 are antiquarian in nature and therefore best left to local historical societies. In the eagerness to reach the more promising lands of the pastoral frontier, the convict interlude and the problems of early culture contact are partially suppressed.[8]

One recurring theme of the early period, however, is that of the enterprising capitalist overcoming the constraints of the command economy and thereby liberating the forces of economic progress. The vital search is for a developing, forward-looking industry with a secure future, and without some of the economic uncertainties and dubious personalities of sealing and whaling.[9] Inevitably the dark, vengeful and melancholic John Macarthur is seen as the first great Australian, and the embodiment of an independent, progressive spirit. The pastoral frontier and the growth of the wool industry provide the first worthy and dynamic themes for the Whig historians. The pastoral frontier was an expanding and prosperous one. Its story told of the taming of an inhospitable environment; a coming to terms with isolation and hardship. The pastoral industry was the forcing ground for the development of a sturdy and distinctive national character.

Such a view of Australia's past therefore creates something of a hiatus between 1788 and the period of frontier expansion. However, the Whig historians of Australia's origins have recently sought to bridge the gap, but within the same tradition. In terms of this explanation the settlement of New South Wales 'was a part of an integrated colonial policy, which was based on the most efficient and extensive exploration programme of any world power'.[10] The engines of the industrial revolution and the impulses of colonial expansion had found a new commercial and imperial role for the new colony, embracing the Indian empire and the trade to China. Before a credible export industry developed in New South Wales, the colony had a grand role to play as some sort of linchpin of Britain's imperial fortunes in the east. In one interpretation, this bridging role extends into the period of the war against Napoleonic France. Frost explained it as follows:

In this circumstance, Britain needed non-European sources of naval and other strategic materials, and bases from which squadrons might operate; and this need meant a strategic role for the infant Colony in New South Wales.[11]

Margaret Steven has recently endorsed this view of the strategic importance of the Botany Bay decision, but has felt an obligation to account for the paucity and ambiguity of the supporting evidence in terms of the ministry's need for secrecy.[12] Before the pastoral frontier there was therefore the equally noble strategic frontier, on which New South Wales made its contribution to the expansion and defence of empire.

In seeking to deny the true origins of European settlement in Australia, or to play down the background of its earliest inhabitants, some historians are erasing important facets of their past. In seeking to ennoble their origins they are in danger of destroying much that is unique and remarkable about Australian history. A settlement founded with the worst possible motives, and in terms of the age, with the worst possible colonists, rapidly overcame these handicaps and developed a healthy society. In spite of imperial neglect and incompetence, Australia became the greatest and most successful experiment in criminal reformation the world has seen. As the bicentenary of the European settlement of Australia draws near it seems appropriate to attempt to put the record straight, and to reinforce the arguments of historians such as Gonner, O'Brien, Manning Clark, Shaw and Bolton who have known the truth all along.

The case presented here therefore reverts to the traditional explanation for the European settlement of New South Wales. During the 1780s a particular combination of circumstances arose to create a penal crisis of unusual and unprecedented proportions in Britain. This crisis had political and ideological repercussions which made it difficult to resolve, and placed the ministry of William Pitt on the horns of a dilemma. Pitt and his colleagues were under strong pressure to reduce government expenditure, but at the same time to relieve the convict burden which was building up in the localities. These pressures, of course, worked in opposite directions, and by 1785 had fostered an atmosphere of desperation in the approach to the convict problem.

In seeking to renew transportation the government cast about widely, and even wildly, for suitable sites for convict colonies. In the process they inevitably considered a variety of private proposals for settlements in what might broadly be termed the 'southern oceans'. These proposals, such as those of Matra, Young and Call, have attracted much attention from the Whig historians of Australia's origins, but the suggestion here is that this attention has not been warranted. Most of the plans sought to exploit the possibilities opened up by Captain Cook's voyages of discovery. In the main they were commercial, and aimed at promoting the interests of their creators, rather than those of government. The schemes were also highly speculative, and even Utopian in character, and very much in the tradition of earlier schemes for the settlement of north and south America. There was also a tradition that governments took such schemes with a grain of salt, which also proved to be the case with the Pitt ministry after 1783.

However, the ministry's own efforts to find a dumping ground for convicts were thwarted at almost every turn. As objections were put forward to one venue after another, the administration became increasingly impatient and desperate. When its penultimate destination, Das Voltas Bay, was ruled out in mid-1786, the ministry reluctantly chose the worst alternative, Botany Bay. In doing so it was aware of the many objections and problems which would be raised by such a choice, and therefore it gave free rein to speculation about the commercial possibilities opened up by the annexation of New South Wales. Such possibilities offered something of a smoke-screen for a decision, which, on its own merits, was almost indefensible.

The preparation of the first fleet, and the early years in New South Wales, made clear the very limited aims of government. The focus was on getting rid of convicts as quickly as possible, and emptying those in county and metropolitan jails into vacant spaces in the prison hulks. There were no attempts to equip the first fleet with any of the men or materials necessary for the development of the much-vaunted commercial or strategic resources. Once the first fleet had arrived in Port Jackson, all ministerial references to flax and naval stores disappeared. The government obviously hoped the English public would forget the whole affair, as indeed the government itself did its best to do.

In selecting Botany Bay as a site for a penal colony strategic considerations had no relevance. In the 1780s Britain was certainly concerned about its traditional areas of imperial interest: the sea routes down the Atlantic and around the Cape of Good Hope, and the navigation of the eastern seas themselves. Some of the sites suggested as convict colonies were adjacent to the sea routes to the east, and offered some limited possibilities for strategic development. New South Wales was not in this category. Geographical common sense, as well as the records of the time, show that Botany Bay was too distant from the sea lanes, and too uncertain of navigation to serve any useful strategic purpose. After the colony had been established, the concern about the passage to the east manifested itself in the same vein as before, without reference to the new territorial acquisition.

New South Wales was just as irrelevant to the defence of the Indian empire itself. It is true, as Frost suggested, that Britain was concerned about the possibility of an Anglo-Dutch alliance aimed at reducing Britain's power in the east, although the scope of the British reaction to this threat has been exaggerated. The departure of the La Perouse expedition did not engender great panic in 1785, and certainly did not change thinking on the convict problem. A French threat in the east was conceived of in very traditional terms, and the response to it involved no strategic innovation. It was a traditional blend of diplomatic effort and bullying in Europe, and strengthening of military power around India and the sea routes to China. The strategic weak points were thousands of miles from

Botany Bay and that lonely outpost was not well placed to strengthen them. In wartime this traditional response produced attacks on the seats of French and Dutch power in the region: Pondicherry, the Île de France, Trincomalee, the Cape of Good Hope and the Dutch East Indies. These were the regions of the greatest French and British vulnerability. No thought was given to incorporating the new settlement at Port Jackson into this eastern strategy, either as a base or as a supplier of naval stores.

Eighteenth-century governments did not adapt quickly to changed situations, and accordingly were slow to adjust their world view. The policy-forming resources available to them were slender, and even the most capable civil servants, such as the Undersecretary at the Home Office, Evan Nepean, could not thoroughly comprehend the range of tasks confronting them. In the normal course of events, precedent acted as the guide to action, but faced with novel situations, administrations often floundered for some time before finding adequate solutions to their problems. Governments and their advisors were therefore largely problem- or crisis-oriented. They responded to political or strategic difficulties and were reactive by nature. Their aptitude for anticipation and planning was slight.[13]

The settlement of New South Wales provides a classic example of this mode of administration. When the convict crisis developed, the first response was to seek guidance in past precedents, and to renew transportation in the traditional mould. As this option closed off, the government sought close parallels to the old system. As this alternative also collapsed, the handling of the question became increasingly desperate and makeshift. New South Wales was the culmination of this regressive process. Only in this sense can the European settlement of Australia be seen as in keeping with the spirit or temper of the age.

Chapter 2

THE CONVICT CRISIS 1775–90

By July 1786 the convict problem in Britain had become so acute that the Pitt government was catapulted into establishing a penal colony at the unlikely site of Botany Bay. To have determined so quickly on so distant a site, with its attendant high supply costs, suggested either an ulterior motive for the settlement or a level of desperation which bordered on panic. There were two reasons for alarm: first, the pressures produced by the growth of the convict population; and second, the immense difficulties in finding a solution to the problem. This chapter will address itself to the first of these issues. The complexity of the issues faced by the government are examined in Chapters 3 and 4.

By the middle of 1786 the Pitt ministry was faced with a dilemma of penal policy which had produced alarming political and social effects. The origins of this dilemma lay in three areas: the breakdown of traditional modes of punishment for felons; changes in the sentencing pattern of felons; and a 'crime wave' in the years after the American War of Independence. Political pressure from the localities, from advocates of penal reform and from advocates of economical government further exacerbated the problem. These pressures were applied moreover to to a young ministry, with an uncertain future and with powerful and articulate opponents. Little attention has been given recently to an examination of the crisis and its role in the foundation of Australia.

The origins of transportation as a form of exile and a punishment for felons are well known, and need not be rehearsed in any detail. Elizabethan legislation had provided for the exile of vagabonds and those addicted to a 'roguish kind of life'. A Privy Council decision of 1601 provided for vagrants to be sent into the army overseas, and subsequently to Newfoundland, the East and West Indies, Spain, the Netherlands, France and Germany.[1] Although it is unlikely that such removals occurred on any scale, these measures established what was to be an important aspect of transportation: the removal from England of what were regarded as worthless and unproductive elements of the population.

Although under the first two Stuarts provision existed for the transportation of felons, it was not general practice until the Restoration, when a series of enactments regularized the procedure and established proper destinations. In the early Hanoverian period the Transportation Act of 1718 established it firmly as a form of punishment suitable for a number of specific felonies. Its use as an alternative to capital punishment can be traced from that time. Normally the sentence handed down by the courts would specify the destination in general terms such as America, or occasionally the West Indies, but as the century progressed, most prisoners were shipped to Maryland or Virginia. On the outbreak of the American War of Independence almost 1000 convicts a year were being sent across the Atlantic, and transportation was the sentence meted out in over 70 per cent of cases.[2]

The increasing reliance on transportation in the eighteenth century can only be understood against the wider background of the British criminal justice system. Eighteenth-century judges had a relatively narrow range of punishments to hand down: corporal punishment, imprisonment, transportation and death. Neither corporal punishment nor imprisonment were the rule for felonies. Corporal punishment was usually reserved for offences such as petty theft, minor assaults, disturbances, industrial disorders and social deviancy; normally the stuff of summary justice where quick, exemplary punishment was required. Imprisonment was inflicted as a short-term punishment of three years or less for similar offences, as well as for perjury, fraud, commercial malpractice or manslaughter. Often the two punishments were used in conjunction. However imprisonment was not a preferred sentence for felonies before 1775, and a recent scrutiny of Old Bailey sentences between 1770 and 1774 revealed that only 2.3 per cent of those convicted were dealt with this way. A study of sentences at Assizes in Surrey between 1736 and 1753 showed that imprisonment accounted for only one per cent of sentences. The equivalent figure for Quarter Sessions was only a little higher at 2.6 per cent.[3]

Incarceration was therefore an uncommon and unpopular punishment in the eighteenth century and the reason is obvious: cost. In a decentralized state such as Britain the financial burden for the construction and maintenance of prisons fell on the localities, and therefore on to the local rates. As a result most county and local prisons were small and often makeshift structures, not designed for long-term prisoners. Jails located in the basement of an old castle, such as at Lancaster, were at least relatively secure, albeit at a high physical cost to the occupants. Often, however, the prison was little more than a few bolted rooms above an inn or county hall. Therefore most were like the Surrey County jail, 'greatly out of repair, too small, unwholesome and unsafe for the prisoners'.[4] Perhaps the condition of the Surrey County jail was a factor in the death of thirty-five people there while awaiting trial between 1736 and 1753.

Most prisoners in county and local jails were awaiting trial or the execution of a sentence. This was regarded as the designed or legitimate function of these facilities. To keep the costs of the establishment low, prisoners were expected to provide for their own subsistence, and the jail keeper drew his (or sometimes her) income largely from fees. Provided upkeep of the jail was kept to a bare minimum the financial burden on the local taxpayers could be maintained at a low level.

The exceptions to this pattern were the debtors' prisons, mostly concentrated in London. Howard's survey of 1776 found that 59.7 per cent of all offenders in prisons were debtors. However debtors were processed by the civil courts, and while incarcerated were maintained at their creditors' expense. Although the number of debtors in prison rose rapidly in the early 1780s, their special character and conditions remove them from the scope of this study.[5]

As neither corporal punishment nor imprisonment were generally used as punishments for felonies, two remain: transportation and death. These were not discrete punishments for particular crimes, but practices intimately related by the peculiar paradoxes of the eighteenth-century criminal justice system. Ironically, the number of transportees increased because the number of crimes for which the death sentence was statutory also increased.

In the years 1688 to 1820 the number of capital offences on the statute book rose from approximately fifty to over 200, to give England the most draconian penal code in Europe. Some recent historians of crime have explained the increase as part of a complex ideological superstructure which preserved the authority, and protected the property, of a ruling elite, through an admixture of terror, majesty and the dispensing of mercy. Certainly the bulk of the capital statutes enacted in the eighteenth century were designed to protect property, and the terror of the gallows was a public and exemplary illustration of the ultimate power of the state.

This system of terror was limited in that it would have been socially and politically unacceptable to carry the operation of the penal process through to the final and awesome conclusion in all possible cases. The death sentence had to be meted out with discretion and a sense of proportion, in order to maintain the appropriate level of terror. If used indiscriminately its credibility would be questioned and popular outrage might result.[6] This discretionary use of the death penalty explained why the number of executions for property offences did not rise with the increase in capital statutes. In the second half of the eighteenth century executions actually fell in number as partial verdicts were were brought in against prisoners, or those sentenced to be hanged had their punishments commuted to transportation.[7] Beattie's study of 328 prisoners convicted of capital property crimes in Surrey between 1736 and 1753 showed that a partial verdict was brought against 149, and 179 more were sentenced to be hanged. Of the latter 87 suffered the final penalty, while 92 were reprieved and transported.[8] Of the total convicted, 220 were eventually transported. When the first fleet sailed for Botany Bay, there were 234 convicts aboard the ships who had originally been sentenced to death but had been spared the gallows.[9] Death and transportation existed therefore as mutually dependent processes reinforcing the complex ideology of eighteenth-century law. Judges were able to apportion sentences in a flexible way to achieve the proper mixture of example, deterrence and retribution. In times of a perceived crime wave the balance would tilt gently in favour of the death penalty, but clearly the general tendency after 1750 was for transportation to be substituted more frequently.

Transportation must be thought of not solely as a substitute for, but also in many senses as the equivalent of, the death penalty. Banishment as well as death removed the guilty from the realm, but it did so in a more humane and perhaps productive way. The general hope was perhaps that these undesirables would be permanently removed from England, and transportation, no less than death, was a purifying process. Secretary of State William Grenville understood this when in 1791 he urged Governor Phillip in New South Wales to discourage expirees from returning to England, as there was 'little reason to hope that any persons of that description will apply themselves here to habits or pursuits, of honest industry'.[10] Many convicts recognized this more than symbolic link between transportation and death when they petitioned to be hanged rather than sent overseas.[11]

As well as playing a necessary part in the ideological functioning of the criminal justice system, transportation was a necessity for financial reasons. One of the great disadvantages of imprisonment already noted was its high cost as part of a system in which no public funds were normally provided for the maintenance of jails. It was not possible to increase the use of imprisonment as a punishment without at the same time greatly increasing the burden on the local rates for the construction and maintenance of jails. Transportation avoided increased costs: it was cheap because it was commercial. The labour of convicts was assigned to the shippers who carried them to the American colonies. At the end of the passage the labour of each convict would be assigned to a settler by indenture. Because the shipper 'sold' this labour at the end of a voyage, and normally to a keen market, the cost of transportation to government was small. At the same time, the 'interest' the shipper had in the cargo, offered some guarantee of the good treatment of the convicts. As a solution to the penal problem, transportation only lightly touched the purses of the landed gentry.

Although transportation was beginning to come under attack

from reformers like Howard by 1775, it is clear that the English criminal justice system had become increasingly dependent upon it as an element in an interconnected penal structure. That structure was savagely and abruptly rent by the outbreak of war with the American colonies.

Between 1769 and 1776 an average of 960 convicts a year were transported to the American colonies, but after 1776 this number had to be provided for in other ways.[12] A proportion of the worst felons could be drafted into the army, but for the remainder the immediate answer was the hulks: a temporary expedient which was to last for more than eighty years. The 'Hulks Act' provided for convicts to be put to hard labour in the Thames, raising sand, gravel and soil, and clearing the water and banks.[13] They were to be housed in worn out transport or naval vessels moored beyond Galleon's Reach. Nominally the hulks were the administrative concern of the justices of Middlesex. In fact, the justices transferred responsibility to the overseer and contractor who supplied the ships and provisioned the prisoners. The first of these contractors was Duncan Campbell, a shipper who had considerable experience of transportation to America. Three months after the passage of the Act he had two ships ready to receive convicts. Although the first two hulks, the *Justitia* and *Censor*, were only supposed to house 380 men between them, the number in each gradually rose until by 1785 there were more than 250 convicts in each.[14] By that year four more hulks and two hospital ships had been added to their number, and their locations had been extended to Plymouth and Portsmouth where the convicts worked on harbour, dockyard and ordnance tasks. The original Hulks Act was limited in operation to one year, but it was frequently renewed and its scope extended.

The hulks were not only a temporary, but also also a partial, expedient. In 1776 they were able to absorb only 60 per cent of those under sentence of transportation at the time. Although the war absorbed some of the convict population through recruitment to the armed forces, a considerable number of convicts requiring accommodation remained.[15] Part of the response was to increase the number of hulks. Another was to increase the number in the hulks until they were dangerously overcrowded: this point had certainly been reached by 1785. A substantial gap remained, and it was filled by the only other penal resource short of hanging: the poorly-financed, insecure and inadequate county and borough jails.

The era of the hulks produced another change: as judges became confused about the status of transportation, they began to adopt imprisonment as a regular form of punishment for felons, especially those convicted of minor property crimes. In part, the reason for sentencing felons to imprisonment was the reluctance of judges to name the American colonies as a place of destination after 1775, and the requirement of the Act that a destination should be stated.

Therefore imprisonment became something of a fall-back option. As a Lancaster magistrate pointed out to the Beauchamp Committee, judges resorted to this alternative without a great deal of thought for the direct consequences of their actions.[16] Nevertheless the consequences soon became obvious. The county and borough jails became desperately overcrowded and for the first time the prisons became places of permanent detention. Ignatieff's figures on the distribution of punishments handed down at the Old Bailey between 1760 and 1794 tell the story.[17]

Individual punishments as a percentage of sentences

	Hulks, Death	Whip, Brand, Transported	Fine	Imprisoned
1760–64	12.7	74.1	12.3	1.2
1765–69	15.8	70.2	13.4	0.8
1770–74	17.0	66.5	14.2	2.3
1775–79	20.7	33.4	17.6	28.6
1780–84	25.8	24.1	15.5	34.6
1785–89	18.5	50.1	13.2	13.3
1790–94	15.9	43.9	11.7	28.3

Although the figures for other forms of punishment show perceptible rises from 1775 onwards, it is with imprisonment that the most dramatic changes occurred, as the number sentenced to transportation declined. Those sentenced in this way became permanent prison residents for their set term of years since there was no capacity to alter their sentence to one of transportation.

The parlous situation in county and borough jails, and on the hulks, was exacerbated sharply after 1782 by external forces which influenced the pattern of crime: a sharp economic decline accompanied by a rise in food prices, and the ending of the war. The price of basic foods such as wheat and bread had risen steadily after 1760, but between 1782 and 1785 they increased sharply, and real wages also fell, as the figures in the following table make clear.[18] The other factor affecting the crime rate in this period was the demobilization following the ending of the war for America. In 1783 about 130 000 men left the services. Once paid off they began their journeys home, sometimes carrying disease with them. As they sought work they added to the unemployed, especially in London where much of the work was only casually or seasonally available. Even the King realized the consequences of this: 'the increase of Highway Robberies has been very great even during the War, and now will naturally increase from the Number of idle persons that this Peace will occasion . . .'.[19] The problem was exacerbated further by the high levels of bankruptcy and business uncertainty at the time.[20]

Wheat and bread prices, and real wages, 1776–86

	Wheat (London) shillings per qtr	Bread (London) pence per lb	Real Wages (1700=100) London	Lancashire
1776	39/4	5.8	98	167
1777	46/11	6.6	90	153
1778	43/3	6.5	96	163
1779	34/8	5.5	105	171
1780	36/9	5.7	98	160
1781	46/0	7.0	98	160
1782	49.3	7.0	85	147
1783	54/3	7.0	88	144
1784	50/4	6.9	95	146
1785	43/1	6.1	93	155
1786	40/1	5.5	96	174

The increase in poverty and unemployment had two linked effects: it increased levels of crime and it increased the burden on the poor rates. From figures of indictments, Beattie has convincingly shown that there was a 'crime wave' in England between 1780 and 1784, and this was characterized by an increase in property crimes in particular. Douglas Hay has recently observed that the combination of demobilization and high food prices made 1783 an especially bad year.[21] The sharpest rise was between 1782 and 1784 and correlates significantly with the rise in the price of basic foods. The predicament of London was highlighted by the increase in the number committed for trial at the Old Bailey between 1783 and 1786, which was forty per cent higher than for the previous three years.[22] Contemporaries were fully aware of the 'crime wave' affecting their society, and there were mixed calls for reform of the penal system and harsher treatment of offenders. In October 1782 Secretary of State Townshend complained to the Duke of Newcastle about the 'frequent Robberies and Disorders of late committed in the Streets of London and Westminster, and Parts adjacent'. He urged that magistrates be sterner in dealing with such outbreaks.[23] The latter call was answered in the traditional resort to terror seen in the upward leap of figures for capital executions between 1780 and 1785. In London and the Home Counties only about one-third of capital convicts received pardons, compared to about two-thirds in the years before the war.[24]

The increased level of criminal indictments in these years placed a further burden on the county and borough jails, and hulks, which were already staggering under the load transferred to them by the ending of transportation and the increased use of imprisonment as a punishment. At the same time as the local authorities were shouldering the financial implications of this change, they were faced with growing pressure on the poor rates generated by the same parlous economic circumstances. A Commons Committee on poor relief suggested in 1786 that the numbers claiming assistance in some parishes had increased by 30 per cent in the previous decade.[25]

Throughout the eighteenth century the English landed gentry had been vigilant in the matter of expenditure at the central and local level. Hints of extravagance or peculation had attracted their ire and produced countless assaults on ministries. The costly American War had, if anything, sharpened their sensitivity to the issue and provided the mainsprings for the Economical Reform movement, and pressure for closer scrutiny of public accounts. Those who contributed most to the net wealth of the community (those with a 'stake in the country') were concerned to see that their outlay was not squandered. But in the early 1780s, when the end of the war offered prospects of reduced expenditure and taxation, the gentry found a new burden imposed upon them in the localities. This was a hot political issue, and given the mood of the times, a political issue of inflammatory proportions, since it occurred at the seat of landed class power and authority. The new Pitt ministry came under powerful and sustained pressure to alleviate this burden on the localities. As this coincided with Pitt's endeavours to extend the central revenue resources so as to be able to reduce the National Debt, the gentry were able to argue that their property was under threat from two directions.[26]

The ending of transportation, more frequent use of imprisonment, the post-war recession, and associated crime wave therefore created problems of crisis proportions. The dimensions of this were apparent in the hundreds of letters which poured in to the Home Office, to individual ministers, and to MPs, requesting a removal of convicts from local jails. The reasons given were desperate overcrowding, the likelihood or actuality of outbreaks of contagious diseases, the likelihood or actuality of riots and escapes, the spread of corruption and immorality, and the fear generated within the local community. There is abundant evidence that these calls for relief represented a great deal more than just local hysteria.

As previously indicated, by 1785 the population of convicts in the hulks greatly exceeded the planned capacity; in cases such as the *Justitia*, by as much as twofold. The position in the jails around the country was no better. The penal reformer John Howard estimated that the prison population of England increased by 73 per cent in the decade after 1776. Newgate, the largest prison in the country, housed 200 inmates in 1750: by 1785 this had increased to over 600. According to its keeper at that time, Richard Ackerman, its population had doubled since 1780 without any increase in the size of the facility.[27] By November 1785 the Newgate situation had reached the point where the Secretary of State had been obliged to move 300 inmates to a new hulk on the south coast.[28] The Surrey

County Jail, described in 1751 as being 'greatly out of repair, too small, unwholesome and unsafe for the prisoners', was in no better condition in 1786, but the number of inhabitants had almost doubled. Between December 1784 and August 1786 the number of convicts in the jail awaiting their sentences of transportation to be carried out, had multiplied three and one-half times.[29] This predicament was very common—between August 1784 and September 1786 there were seventy-seven requests for removal of convicts from county and borough jails for reasons of overcrowding. These requests came from forty-seven different institutions.[30]

Jail fever (or typhus) and distemper were endemic in the jails of eighteenth-century England, and were the product of insanitary conditions in which lice, as the vector, flourished. The hulks and jails provided an ideal environment for the propagation of fever, and the dirty and often hungry convicts were ideal hosts. Smallpox and other contagious diseases were also common. In the years after 1782 fever outbreaks were reported from jails all over the country, and from the hulks as well. Eleven died in the Ilchester jail in August 1783, and twenty-two more in February of the following year. A fever in the Somerset jail in November 1783 carried off several prisoners, the jailor, his wife, and a local doctor.[31] In the drastically crowded Maidstone jail in January 1784, with over one hundred prisoners, a 'putrid' fever killed twenty-eight and left many others dangerously ill. In September eighty-five convicts on the ship *Sally* contracted typhus.[32]

One notorious jail in the kingdom was at Gloucester, in an old castle by a river. All male convicts were confined in one dank room, and when a group of MPs visited the prison in 1783 they found forty convicts chained together by their foot fetters. In this condition they lived, ate and slept. There was no infirmary or provision for the sick. An outbreak of jail fever at Christmas 1778 killed eight, and a worse bout in 1783 killed fourteen; others discharged from the prison spread the fever outside its walls.[33] Confining disease within the jail walls was a nigh impossible task given the movement in and out of eighteenth-century prisons, as the Gloucestershire case illustrated. News of outbreaks spread panic and fear through communities adjacent to jails and hulks, and produced loud calls for the removal of felons. No doubt hysteria generated in this way was as contagious as many diseases, but the public memory had reference to sufficient examples to give edge to the fears. In May 1780 typhus carried by Newgate prisoners spread to the Old Bailey, killing forty persons including the Lord Mayor, two Judges and some court officials. Sixty-two prisoners died in Newgate that year.[34] As early as July 1782 Shelburne pointed out the problems of public concern about overcrowding in a memorandum for Townshend, his successor in the Home Office: 'the Judges have repeatedly remonstrated, and the Hulks are in such a State, which will excite a Publick

Clamor'.[35] Naval vessels moored near the the hulks at Portsmouth and Plymouth regularly contracted typhus and smallpox, creating scares in the naval ports themselves. In 1787 typhus was even carried on board the transport ship *Alexander* which was part of the first fleet to Botany Bay. Although the convicts were removed and the ship was cleaned, this did not destroy the infection. Ten of the fifteen convicts who died on the first fleet by the time it reached Rio were on board the *Alexander*.[36] The fear generated by such events was the propellant for many requests for the removal of convicts after 1782.

Between August 1784 and August 1786, twenty-nine different authorities expressed fears of riots or escapes to the Home Office. The same records report fifteen escapes from jails or hulks over this period, but there is good reason to believe that this represented only major outbreaks involving violence.[37] The lax security at most jails coupled with the freedom of access to friends and relations, meant that it was relatively easy for prisoners to escape if they were determined to do so. Only in substantial castles like Lancaster, York and Gloucester, where convicts were kept in the dungeons, could any sort of security be guaranteed. These, however, were the prisons with the worst reputations for harbouring jail fever.[38]

Escapes and riots inevitably created fear in local populations and this was manifested once again in frequent requests for removal. In November 1784 the Lord Mayor of London urged that the guard on the hulks on the Thames be strengthened, as he anticipated that demobilized and unemployed sailors would set the convicts free and destroy the hulks. He reminded the Undersecretary of State of the damage such sailors had done during the Gordon riots, when they were thought to be among those who had set fire to Newgate jail, then in the process of reconstruction.[39]

Considering the squalor and crowding of the jails, riots and escapes were inevitable. Most borough and county jails had no facilities for exercising inmates or providing forms of labour outside the walls. Prisoners therefore were closely confined and normally chained. Convicts on the hulks worked during the day, but on an irregular basis. They were also chained, and while on board slept between decks on tiered platforms no more than twenty inches wide, and without sufficient headroom.[40] In the first two years of the hulks 176 convicts died—twenty-eight per cent of those housed aboard them. The first substantial revolt occurred only three months after the first vessels were commissioned, when men seized the arms chest on the *Justitia* and escaped on a boat. There was another escape by twenty-two men shortly after this, and a major rebellion by 150 convicts in September 1778, when three were killed and over twenty wounded.[41]

Conditions in prisons were so bad that the inmates not only rioted and attempted to escape, they petitioned the Secretary of State. In

1783 prisoners at Durham requested a review of their position, and the provision of new clothing. In May 1786 convicts in typhus-infested Lancaster jail, which housed nearly seventy inmates, forwarded a similar petition. The inmates of Southwark also sought redress this way.[42] Perhaps the saddest petition was that composed by the eleven transportees in Leicester jail which was forwarded to the Secretary of State by the Grand Jury of the County in July 1785. These men had been chained in stone cells on a bare ration of bread for three years, without having proper exercise. They begged that their sentences be put into execution.[43]

One other obvious pressure needs to be mentioned: that from reformers seeking a change in the criminal justice system. Even before the American War, men such as Sir John Fielding, John Howard and William Eden had pointed to the failings of the system, and particularly of the death sentence and transportation. Following the ideas of Beccaria, they pressed for less arbitrary and more certain punishments which were graded according to the seriousness of the crime. After the war this call was reinforced by the voices of Bentham, Onesiphorous Paul, Blackstone, and Colquhuon. They placed their faith in penitentiary houses where in solitary cells the convicts could be put to work and given time to reflect on their sins. The Penitentiary Act of 1779 was to provide the mechanism of the changes they wanted. However, without central government funding and support, it was a weak instrument.

Nevertheless, pressure from the reformers placed the government in an invidious position as any perceived failure in the existing system strengthened the argument for change. As the jails and hulks became pestilential and overflowed, and the costs of penal administration rose, the reformers began to sharpen their knives.

There is ample evidence that the Pitt ministry viewed the problems of the prisons and the hulks with the utmost concern, and for three years they desperately sought a remedy. In May 1784 the situation in the Exeter jail became so dangerous that Lord Sydney ordered one of the transports at Plymouth, which was preparing to ship home Hanoverian troops, to be appropriated for the housing of eighty-five convicts and an armed guard.[44] These convicts eventually ended up on the hulk *Dunkirk*. In answer to a request from the Mayor of Hull for prisoners in his jail to be moved to the hulks, Sydney replied: 'The crowded State of the several prisons near this Metropolis as well as the temporary Places of Confinement is such that not a Person can at Present be admitted'.[45] In the same month he dealt in a similar way with a request from Lord Robert Spencer concerning the Oxford Jail. He wished to help, but pointed out: 'the great difficulty which has for some Years past existed of carrying the Sentence of Transportation into Execution has I am sorry to say, been a means of crowding all the Gaols and Places of confinement in and near this Metropolis as well as the Hulks in the

River Thames'.[46] The emphasis on London was a sign of the fears about public order in the aftermath of the Gordon riots. The preamble to the draft plan to send 150 convicts to the Island of Lemain in the Gambia stated that the jails in the Kingdom were: 'so crowded that the greatest danger is to be apprehended, not only from their Escape, but from infectious Distemper which may be hourly expected to break out amongst them'.[47] Although the same preamble was used for the orders for Botany Bay some eighteen months later, there is no reason to believe that the declaration was hollow or meaningless.

In November 1785 the problems of overcrowding at the recently rebuilt Newgate prison became so critical that the Secretary of State was again obliged to take remedial action. Three hundred convicts were ordered to be removed to the hulk *Fortunee* at Portsmouth where they were to be employed on the ordnance work at Langston Harbour. Work was also to be found for 200 of the healthy convicts on the *Dunkirk* at Plymouth. As Sydney explained to the Lords of the Treasury, the 'Gaols are in so crowded a State that it is absolutely necessary for the Public Safety that this Measure should be carried into Execution'.[48]

There is little doubt that 1786 saw the crisis at its most acute since the war. The government's search for a solution to the problem became frenetic. There were fifty-six different requests for removal that year from Grand Juries, sheriffs, under-sheriffs, mayors, judges, town clerks and jailors. Eight of these requests were in response to Home Office demands for information. The year began badly with the spreading of fever from the hulk *Firm* at Portsmouth to the Naval Hospital at Haslar. Dr Lind, in charge of the hospital, reported patients with delirium, purple spots, livid discolourations, gangrene and discharges of blood—a lurid reference to the presence of typhus. Although Sydney was informed, little could be done pending the search for a suitable African site for the disposal of the transportees, and the examination of plans for the employing of the convicts locally. Early in the year the government seemed to have decided to transport the convicts at all costs, irrespective of the information brought back by the *Nautilus* expedition. Various sets of estimates were gathered and contingency plans produced.[49]

It is apparent that the pressure of the penal problem was beginning to produce threatening political repercussions for the government as the pace of requests for removal quickened in April and May. The actual shape of this pressure is evident in the activities of two Devon MPs, John Rolle and John Pollexfen Bastard. Both of these men were independents, Rolle being described by the historians of Parliament as 'A completely independent country gentleman, strong-minded, original, and unpredictable'. He was an influential member of the St Albans Tavern group and just the sort of MP whom governments needed to cultivate actively. Pitt was not so assured of his position in the House that he could lightly contemplate the move of a number of independents towards the Foxite ranks on any issue.[50] Both Rolle and Bastard had on occasion voted against the Pitt ministry, and at the beginning of 1786 both were opposing the Duke of Richmond's plans for the fortification of the dockyards at Portsmouth and Plymouth.[51] Both men were urging the government to take prompt action to renew transportation, and of course both men had hulks in their electorates. In early May, Rolle supplied information on the convicts in the crowded Devon Jail, and took the opportunity of badgering the Home Office:

It is my earnest Wish & the Directions I have rec'd from my Constituents to use every Endeavour to have the Sentences inforc'd by sending them out of the Kingdom—Mr Pitt told me yesterday Preparations were making for this Purpose of which he will write me more particularly tomorrow to transmit for the Satisfaction of my Constituents.[52]

The following day Pitt wrote to Rolle assuring him of the ministry's intention of acting promptly on this matter:

Tho I am not at this Moment able to state to You the Place, to which any Number of the Convicts will be sent, I am able to assure You that Measures are taken for procuring the Quantity of Shipping necessary for conveying above a thousand of them. And I have every reason to suppose that all the Steps necessary for the removal of at least that Number, may be compleated in about a Month. The Plan may I am in hopes, afterwards be extended to whatever farther Number may be found requisite.[53]

This does not reflect a decision by Pitt to build a base to serve as a place of refreshment for India ships, and as a strategic outpost to the subcontinent.[54] It must indeed have been a cavalier sense of strategy which could recognize such a need without reference to geography. Pitt's letter was, in fact, an answer to a specific request from a powerful MP who held considerable sway with the independent country gentry. On 7 May Rolle wrote to Townshend informing him of Pitt's letter, and the authority the Prime Minister had given to 'communicate to the public'. At least two shipping contractors were given the same information, since they wrote to Nepean asking for details of the scheme.[55]

Because of the desperate situation in the jails in May and June, it is apparent that the Pitt ministry drew up contingency plans for the transportation of between 600 and 1000 convicts. These plans were not geared to one particular site, or to any purpose other than the disposal of convicts. In these months Nepean sought estimates for particular aspects of the project from various merchants. These were forwarded to the Treasury with the instruction to keep the question of sites open.[56] This points to the determination of government to dispose of the convicts at all costs over the forthcoming summer. Forward planning of this was to go ahead with sufficient flexibility so that it could be adapted to a number of locations.

As is now known, the Das Voltas Bay expedition of 1786 returned with bad reports of the proposed site. Caught between two stools, the government was pushed to desperate measures. It moved therefore to the only immediate alternative: Botany Bay.

The first fleet for New South Wales was intended to carry 788 convicts, most of whom would be removed from the hulks. However it is obvious that this sailing would have only partially relieved pressure on the overburdened penal system. Although the 'crime wave' had receded by the beginning of 1787, it will be remembered that almost 1000 convicts a year were transported to the American Colonies in the five years before Independence. The first fleet therefore removed barely a year's supply. The ministry also took the sensible precaution of holding back shipments of more transportees until favourable reports were received from New South Wales. This meant a delay of at least two years between the dispatch of the first fleet and the preparation of another, during which time a backlog of convicts would obviously build up.

In fact the second fleet did not leave before July 1789. It was inevitable in these circumstances that the acute pressure which had lead to the Botany Bay decision would continue for a few years after the decision was made. In selecting felons for the first fleet the government had also drawn heavily from the hulks and the jails in the London area, somewhat at the expense of other parts of the country.

Before the end of 1787 the familiar signs of overcrowding and disease began to manifest themselves again in the jails. In October the Home Office arranged for the establishment of another hulk. Expenditure was approved by the Treasury for one to house 230 convicts.[57] By October of the following year there were 2800 felons awaiting transportation and the old problems were apparent in all their forms.[58] After convicts had been removed from the hulks to the transports of the first fleet, their places were taken up by more felons from the county jails. These brought with them the usual crop of diseases, and in May 1788 typhus swept through the hulks at Langston Harbour, Portsmouth, killing several men. A sloop was converted rapidly into a hospital ship for infected survivors. Accommodation problems were exacerbated in May when the hulk *Dunkirk* became so leaky that all her convicts had to be moved out while she was repaired.[59] In spite of the removal of 300 convicts from Newgate in November 1785, and more for the first fleet, by October 1788 that prison was accommodating 750, and overcrowding had reached an explosive point, especially for female convicts.[60]

The requests for removal after 1787 were particularly strong from regions distant from London which had not been substantially relieved by the first fleet. The Carlisle jailer sought help in May

1789, but getting little response, he enlisted the weighty assistance of Sir William Lowther, MP for the County of Cumberland. Lowther at least managed to elicit a reply from Grenville, the new Secretary of State, and was assured that there was 'no County in England which is not at present subject to the inconvenience of which you complain'. No more transportees could be removed to the hulks 'as they are already so crowded that any addition to their number would infallibly produce infectious disorders among them'.[61] It is apparent that these distant areas had been to some extent sold short.

This was also the situation in Scotland. In February 1787, Sydney had told the Lord Justice Clerk that the penal problem was well in hand, and Scotland's situation would soon be attended to. There is little evidence that this happened. By October the Lord Advocate was complaining about the crisis in the jails and the escalating scale of the problem. The following January the Lord Provost and magistrates of Glasgow asked for their transportees to be removed, pointing at the same time to the dubious legality of informally changing a sentence from one of transportation to one of imprisonment. Three months later the magistrates of Aberdeen put in a similar plea.[62] In February 1789 the shipping contractor William Richards suggested that government had given prime attention to the London and Home Circuit jails where the political pressure and concern for public order were greatest.[63]

In the months immediately before the sailing of the second fleet for New South Wales, the convict problem rose to another peak. The Maidstone jail, which was already in a crisis situation in April 1786 when 103 inmates were detained, was in an even more parlous state by October 1789 with 120 inmates. A Kent magistrate explained to Nepean that the jail was bursting at the seams and two recently escaped convicts had not been recaptured. The county had been reticent about pressing the government in the past, 'knowing the difficulties that the Executive Power have met with in finding out a proper place to transport the Convicts'.[64] The Keeper of the Lincoln jail asked Sir Joseph Banks to exert his influence to have prisoners removed from the county. These felons were ill-fed, ill-housed and ill-clothed, and not unnaturally the keeper feared that riots were imminent. Nevertheless the county was not relieved by the sailing of the second fleet, and the keeper was still pressing Banks on the question a year later, and complaining of the lack of response from the Secretary of State.[65]

The second and third fleets, and then the onset of the Revolutionary Wars, gradually relieved the pressure on the jails, although the hulks continued to house between 700 and 800 convicts until the Peace of Amiens. These were soon greatly outnumbered by prisoners of war sharing similar accommodation. Eventually the central government began to accede to pressure for proper penitentiaries, and in place of the symbiotic deterrents of death and transportation, a more comprehensive, but less interdependent system based on an extended range of penal resources was established.

This chapter has illustrated that the convict problem in all its dimensions had become particularly grave by 1786. This was in itself sufficient justification for a government decision which, without any other suitable explanation, could be seen as almost entirely irrational. The ending of transportation to America of itself posed enormous problems, not only for the various jails of England, but also for a penal system which was administratively and ideologically dependent upon this punishment. In the early 1780s a number of other forces converged to exacerbate this dilemma until it became a crisis of great social and political dimensions. The post-war depression and demobilization, the crime wave of 1782–5, and the financial pressure on the counties and landed class, combined to make the disposal of transportees a vital issue. The requests for removal of convicts which flooded into the Home Office from sheriffs, MPs, mayors, magistrates and jailors were more than just ritual pleas for the ending of an everyday burden. They were manifestations of critical problems of overcrowding, disease and public order. Insofar as these problems gave rise to genuine public fears about contagion and riot, they had a political dimension which had considerable significance for the Pitt ministry. The behaviour of the ministry in the face of this crisis suggested a degree of panic, and a preparedness to clutch at desperate solutions without adequate investigation of the consequences. Over the period after 1782, the government considered many wild and wonderful plans for the solution of the penal problem, most of which had little in common other than the possibility of reward for their promoters. The nature and influence of these plans are the subject of the next chapter.

Chapter 3

PRIVATE ENTERPRISE AND THE SOUTHERN OCEANS

The next two chapters focus on interconnected aspects of the decision to transport convicts to Botany Bay. This chapter assesses the various private plans for the settlement of Australasia after 1776. Chapter 4 examines the efforts of the Pitt ministry to locate a suitable site for the dumping of felons sentenced to transportation. Although these questions must initially be considered separately, by 1784 they began to overlap as the promoters of private commercial enterprises modified their schemes to conform to government requirements for a solution to the convict problem. It is argued here that the prime motive of the originators of these private schemes—men such as Matra, Young and Call—was self-interest, and that there are therefore misconceptions and dangers involved in in using the private plans as indicators of government intentions and motivation. These men were essentially entrepreneurs and promoters, petitioning rather than advising government. However the commercial inspiration of their original proposals has given a misleadingly commercial tinge to the debate about the origins of European settlement in New South Wales. It is shown here that many of these private promoters were extremely fickle in their attachment to particular sites for settlement, and modified their plans to suit what they believed to be the prevailing prejudices in the Home Office, or in the Pitt ministry, at any particular time.

Captain Cook's voyages had stimulated European interest in the Pacific, and awakened entrepreneurs to the possibility of its commercial exploitation. Natural scientists had accompanied each voyage and their reports and specimens had reinforced the possibility of developing numerous resources in the region. Various landfalls were identified as sites suitable for European settlement, and for the production of European crops and livestock. Eventually, of course, many of these commercial and settlement opportunities were to be exploited. Whalers and sealers moved into the Pacific. Adventurers headed to the north-west coast of America in search of sea otter furs. Ships were sent on voyages to gather the Tahitian bread-fruit and other tropical products.[1] A convict colony was established on the impressive shores of Port Jackson.

Such interest in the Pacific region had its natural origins in the search for the fabled southern continent. Somewhere in the southern hemisphere there existed a continent counterbalancing the mass of northern countries. Faith in this chimera was strong from the sixteenth century onwards, but was stimulated anew by the great eighteenth century voyages of exploration.[2] The visionary aspect of many of the private plans considered here owed much to the original conception of the southern continent. Not only was this land mass to be a spatial counterpart to that in the other hemisphere, but it was to be a material one as well. Everything that society had current need of, or desire for, was there in abundance. Just as in an age when bullion and spices were at a premium did it contain those commodities, so in an age of industrial revolution and naval power did it offer prospects for cotton, indigo, metals, and spars. There was an Arcadian quality to the plans of these promoters, and they were as much a part of a literary tradition as a scientific one. They offered an opportunity of solving problems in the mother country while exploiting a bounteous and rich environment elsewhere.

Cook's voyages had a particularly stimulating effect on such thought. Perhaps motivated by indignation at his failure to get command of the *Endeavour* voyage in 1768, the geographer Alexander Dalrymple put forward a commercial plan backed by Benjamin Franklin. Dalrymple proposed to equip a speculative voyage to New Zealand in which food, European livestock, iron and implements would be exchanged for flax and other natural products likely to be useful in England. A ship of the cat-built *Endeavour* type would be employed, and Dalrymple would command the expedition on behalf of the subscribers. It was calculated that £15 000 would be sufficient to fund the plan.[3] Failing to arouse much enthusiasm for this proposal, in the following year Dalrymple sought to interest Lord North in the colonization of the mythical Isla Grande, thought to lie somewhere in the middle of the south Atlantic. This island would supply provisions for the West Indies and serve as a base for vessels on their way to India or the Pacific. Isla Grande, he wrote to North:

cannot fail of being a very temperate and pleasant Country, in a situation very favourable for carrying on the whale and other Fisheries, and also for the prosecution of any Commerce in the Countries to the South.[4]

These countries were of course contained within the main object of Dalrymple's concern, *Terra Australis Incognita*, lying a mere five degrees south of the Isla Grande itself. In the geographer's view this continent was destined to fulfil the same role as the most prosperous of the North American colonies, which England was at that time in the process of losing. Once again, Dalrymple hoped to command any expeditions which North endorsed.

At about the same time another frustrated traveller was thinking of a scientific and commercial voyage to the southern oceans. In May 1772 Joseph Banks had stormed out of Cook's second expedition because of disagreements over the fitting of the *Resolution*. Vanity and foolishness had temporarily overwhelmed him. It was perhaps pique which then drove him to formulate his own South Sea expedition. Want of promoters led to the abandonment of that plan, but Banks would have some expedition however, and that year he set off with Gore, his intended commander, for Iceland.[5]

In 1776 Banks's name was connected with another expedition which was to be led by Captain Charles Clerke, recently returned from Cook's second voyage. A vessel was to carry out goods to the Pacific and restore the Tahitian, Omai, to his native land. On the return voyage a cargo of breadfruit and other esculent plants was to be loaded for transhipment to the West Indies and other British colonies.[6]

During the American War of Independence all such private enterprise plans had to be set aside because of the additional risks involved from enemy ships. Nevertheless, a tradition of speculative plans for voyages to the southern oceans was already established, in which commercial and strategic elements were combined. Cook's third voyage from 1776 to 1780 was insulated from hostilities by a guarantee of free passage by the Americans and later the French. Although its primary concerns were not commercial, it promoted further interest in the Pacific, particularly because of the knowledge brought back to England about the lucrative trade in the skins of the sea otter, *Enhydra lutris*. It appeared likely that once the war was over many private entrepreneurs would want to exploit the commercial potential revealed by Cook's discoveries.

It was inevitable that when such schemes did emerge after the Peace of 1783, they would be linked either with Cook 'veterans' or men with a knowledge of Indian and East Indian waters. Such backgrounds gave a particular flavour and global dimension to the sort of schemes which emerged. The proponents had the capacity to blend successfully strategic and commercial possibilities; to think flexibly about various sites and the connections between them and vital areas of British interest. They were familiar with the literature of discovery and the sea routes of the world. Natural products of far-off lands were automatically seen as commercial assets awaiting exploitation. Their seafaring experience gave them the imagination and factual material to craft schemes that would mesh with government needs. However, unless they were men like Sir Joseph Banks, with a proven track record of liaison with government, the ideas of these men provide a most unreliable guide to the intentions of the ministries of the day.

Apart from the voyage of the *Swallow* in 1783, the first planned commercial venture into the southern oceans after the American War was again linked with the name of Banks.[7] One of his protégés, James Mario Matra, was in London in 1783 seeking jobs and opportunities. He picked up reports of two schemes for expeditions to the South Pacific. The one in which Banks, Sandwich, Lord Mulgrave and a Mr Colman were involved was destined for New South Wales. The other, sponsored by Sir George Young and Mr Jackson, was destined more generally for the South Seas. Both were apparently to be speculative ventures financed by subscription.[8] Banks may have lost enthusiasm for this scheme after having his fingers burnt from investment in the East India vessel *Bessborough*. Her last voyage made a loss, and when the hull was sold it realized less than anticipated.[9]

Matra had sought a part in Banks's proposed scheme because his search for useful employment was not going well. As he told Banks, he 'would prefer embarking in such a scheme to anything much better than what I am likely to get in this Hemisphere'. When this enterprise came to nothing, Matra decided to float his own, using Banks's patronage. On 23 August 1783 he wrote to Lord North, the Secretary of State for Home and Colonial affairs, seeking government support for an alternative plan.

Matra proposed a settlement in New South Wales which would have a strategic and commercial purpose, and also be a refuge for American Loyalists. Because of its location and size, both tropical products such as sugar and spice, and temperate crops would flourish there. Naval stores would be procured from New Zealand: a country mentioned in the same breath, as though the Tasman Sea was little more of an obstacle than the English Channel. Matra apparently had scant regard for the monopolies of the East India and South Sea Companies, for he saw New South Wales as the centre of an Asian/Pacific trading network, involving the spice, fur and China tea trade. His vision was anything but modest. Not only would New South Wales become a substitute for the American colonies, but from there Britain could flail about at the Dutch and Spanish empires in Asia and South America, intercept the Manila galleons 'laden with the Treasures of the West', and dominate the Pacific hemisphere.[10]

As with so many other plans of this type, Matra's scheme had an Arcadian quality to it. New South Wales, of which he had but the briefest acquaintance, was a land of milk and honey with all the qualities which Dalrymple had predicted for the great southern continent itself. No disadvantages or problems were envisaged; no limits on settlement could be imagined. The scheme was visionary and impractical, as Lord North and his fellow ministers would surely have realized.

Presumably Matra showed this plan to Charles James Fox as well, since he had already sought that politician's assistance in connection with other forms of employment.[11] And employment was the central feature of Matra's scheme, for he was suggesting either an initial survey of New South Wales, or an immediate colonizing expedition which he would command. It is difficult to imagine what he thought his qualifications for such a mission might be. Unfortunately, his carefully developed links with the coalition then in power availed him little, for already by the end of August Fox and North were becoming aware of the need to seek more secure props for their ministry. They were also having sufficient difficulty formulating legislation for the administration of one empire without attempting to found another.

After the fall of the Fox–North Coalition in December 1783, Matra was obliged to rebuild his political bridges, and by some time in March of the following year, he had approached the new Secretary of State for Home affairs, Lord Sydney. The latter was already grappling with the convict problem, for the 'Hulks Act' of 1779 was due for renewal, and as the Solicitor General remarked 'No place had yet been found to which convicts under such a sentence could be sent'.[12] It was as a response to a question from Sydney that Matra modified the original plan by way of an appendix, to incorporate the idea of a convict colony. The chief attraction of his argument was cost. For somewhat obscure reasons he believed that the expense of a New South Wales convict colony would be 'absolutely imperceptible, comparatively with what criminals have hitherto cost government'.[13] He envisaged the felons becoming instant farmers; obedient, productive, and skilled on the land. Transport and provisioning costs do not seem to have figured in his calculations. Not surprisingly, the government paid him scant attention at this stage.

Matra obviously saw convicts as devices for attracting government support, rather than as the real reason for a settlement.[14] During 1784 he kept up pressure on the ministry on this basis, elaborating and developing his plan for the market. In August he even sought to elicit the support of Fox: surely at this stage a sign of desperation, since the latter was in Opposition.

In the second half of 1784 the convict problem began to press very heavily on the government. An attempt to land felons in Honduras and Newfoundland had failed, and Caribbean and North American sites at that time seemed to present overwhelming difficulties because of the feelings of the local populations.[15] By this time there was also considerable public awareness of the government predicament, and suggestions old and new began to flow into the ministry.

Many of these schemes referred to convicts as an afterthought,

the prime concern in each case being the employment of the promoter. Naval Captain Edward Thompson recommended the occupation of the island of São Tomé off the West African coast. This
could be developed as a plantation settlement, a base, and a convict
colony. Meeting little success with this idea, he then floated a similar
project for the South American colonies of Demerara and Berbice,
and Essequibo, which could be acquired from the Dutch.[16] Thompson was rather fickle in his attachment to such proposals, for in May
1785 he argued before the Beauchamp Committee against West
African sites because of the wild natives, tropical sun, and danger
to trade through piracy. On the other hand, this change may have
been due to his recent attachment to a more disinterested solution
to the crime wave and the convict problem. In April 1785 he reported to Sydney on his observations following regular attendance
at Tyburn hangings. From the last statements of convicts he had
divined a terror of dissection. He therefore recommended that this
should follow all executions because of its power of deterrence.[17]

In the course of the second half of 1784 more remarkable plans
surfaced. One of the most indefatigable promoters was Admiral Sir
George Young. Young's naval experience extended to East Indian,
American, Caribbean and African waters. Between 1783 and 1788
he let hardly a year go by without having a settlement proposition
of some sort before government. Unfortunately, as he lamented in
February 1793, the government did not always do him the honour
of a consultation upon vital subjects such as New South Wales.[18] At
some time in 1783 Young sought government support for a British
colony on Madagascar, but he had surprisingly overlooked the
charter of the East India Company. His name was also associated at
this time with the expedition to the South Seas in which Banks and
Sandwich were involved.

Sometime late in 1784 Young became more materially involved
in New South Wales when he forwarded to Pitt a scheme for a
colony there. This plan went through some modification in the
course of 1785.[19] Young's plans were so close to those of Matra that
it is scarcely worthwhile considering them separately. Since Matra's
appeared first, it may be reasonable to assume that Young's was
derivative, which raises the question of why he bothered to submit
it at all. Like Matra he saw New South Wales as a country able to
produce almost any crop. The first version also highlighted the New
Zealand flax, the China trade, proximity to the spice islands, and
the possibility of trade with (or war upon) the Dutch and Spanish
colonies. Again, as in the Matra plan, settlers would be provided
from among the American Loyalists, and the inhabitants of China.
The convict possibility was tacked on as if an afterthought, without
any modification of the stated need for other types of settler. This
was another plan intended to be all things to all men. The cost of
the whole undertaking would be £3000—the same as Matra's esti-

mate—but although this was to include the supply of three ships, only fifty felons would go on the first fleet. That a maximum of only 140 convicts would be taken out each year pointed to the true nature of this scheme as one for settlement. Even accepting this, however, the estimate of £3000 was ludicrously low.

Between the end of 1784 and April 1785 Young's plan was considered by the Pitt ministry, being modified each time to accommodate it more to the perceived needs of government. As Atkinson has shown, convicts featured more and more prominently, and the trading aspect seemed to fade into less significance.[20] But in adapting the plan in this way, Young was in great danger of rendering himself unnecessary to the plan; or, at the least, rendering the plan unprofitable. Like Matra, he too sought lucrative employment, and his initial proposal was laced with words which have a characteristically eighteenth century ring: 'Had I command of this Expedition . . .'. A settlement inhabited solely by convicts was not to his liking, and in June 1785 he proposed another plan for a commercial settlement—this time on Norfolk Island. In this enterprise he was associated with a promoter whose virtuosity almost exceeded his own. His name was John, later Sir John, Call.

Call's formative years were spent in India. As Frost has shown, his experience there provided the generative force for many of his later designs. In 1762 he put forward a plan for the invasion of Île de France. In 1779 he proffered a plan for attacking Spanish American colonies. At about this time he propounded a scheme for giving Plymouth dockyard a better water supply. 1784 was his most productive year. He offered several plans: a trading expedition to the north-west coast of America, a scheme for reducing the East India Company debts in India, and, according to Frost, a plan for shipping convicts to New South Wales.[21] The following year he joined with Young in the proposal to colonize Norfolk Island, and when the government seemed determined on sending convicts to Das Voltas Bay, he sought employment in that enterprise.[22] Two years after the decision to settle Botany Bay, he joined with Young again in renewing the settlement plan for Norfolk Island.[23]

The frailties of old age and blindness could not sap Call's creative energies. In 1800, the penultimate year of his life, he was urging on Dundas the settlement of the island of Socotra in the Indian Ocean, and the land either side of the Bar el-Mandeb at the mouth of the Red Sea. In most of these schemes, including those for New South Wales and Norfolk Island, Call sought a major role for himself. Unfortunately this great fertility of ideas went largely to waste.

Without any good reason, Frost dates Call's plan for New South Wales to August 1784, placing it before the crucial Beauchamp Committee enquiry into the convict problem. The copy in the Home Office records which he cites is undated, but appears with a body of other documents which the government was viewing in 1786, all relating to the problems of disposing of transportees. The other plans included one for employing the convicts in the Woolwich Rope Yard, and another for using them in Scottish coal mines.[24] Although these were suggestions already on file, the actual dating of Call's proposal is conjectural, as must be the statement that it was addressed to Pitt. This uncertainty is crucial, since it is important to know whether Call's plan emerged before, after, or in conjunction with that of Young. It cannot be determined where it stood in relation to Call's testimony before the Beauchamp Committee in April 1785.[25]

Call's plan for New South Wales was similar in its essentials to that of Young, and bearing their collaboration on the Norfolk Island proposal in mind, it is fair to assume they were versions of each other. Considering Young's indebtedness to Matra, it is difficult to escape the impression that in examining these schemes one is travelling in ever decreasing circles. The loss of the American colonies defined the need; Cook provided the inspiration and example; spices, flax and commerce were the rewards. The settlement would be useful either for Loyalists or convicts. Call, quite naturally, wanted to be part of any enterprise which might eventuate. It was all familiar, including the geographical vagueness which was characteristic of the schemes of Matra and Young.

In December 1784 the Pitt ministry set out to review the possible location for a convict colony. Sites as far apart as Cape Coast Castle and Bencoolen were considered: the ministry also looked at New South Wales.[26] In their consideration of the plans brought forward, there was no mention of strategy or trade as objects of value in themselves. The sole consideration appeared to be convicts. The evidence on New South Wales was drawn from Banks's testimony before the 1779 Bunbury Committee on Felons, and from the plans of Matra and Young. All schemes save the West African one were rejected. Lord Howe, the First Lord of the Admiralty, believed that the isolation of New South Wales made it an impractical site, because of the great sailing times involved.[27] Although the Solicitor General, Pepper Arden, was a little more positive about it, this was solely because it seemed to him to be 'the most likely method of effectually disposing of convicts'. He was nevertheless 'totally ignorant of the probability of the success of such a scheme'. This does not seem a strong recommendation.[28]

During the proceedings of the Beauchamp Committee, which are discussed in the following chapter, it became clear that the government was focusing its attention on an African site; eventually Das Voltas Bay. John Call was not so committed to a convict colony in New South Wales that he forebore offering himself for a Das Voltas Bay settlement, but for twelve months private promoters abandoned the notion of pursuing a convict plan for Botany Bay. There were simply no rewards to be obtained. This was presumably the reason why in June 1785 Young and Call sought government and East India Company approval for a straightforward commercial settlement on Norfolk Island.

This particular proposal requires consideration for two reasons. First, in putting forward their scheme Young and Call raised the question of producing naval stores for India: one of the crucial elements in the arguments of Blainey and Frost about the origins of Botany Bay. Second, the plan produced a withering rejoinder from Alexander Dalrymple on behalf of the East India Company.

Young and Call wanted the sole right to found a settlement on Norfolk Island and 'other small Islands adjacent', for the purposes of cultivating and manufacturing flax, and for supplying masts to East India country ships and naval forces in the east. Atkinson has suggested that they saw the colony as a potential supplier to the convict colony at Botany Bay, but while this may have been true of the 1788 version of the plan, it could hardly apply to that of 1785, which came at a time when the government had swung away from a New South Wales site.[29]

Dalrymple's opinion of this proposal was drawn up for the guidance of the Court of Directors of the East India Company. The idea of supplying flax and masts for the Indian market was smartly dismissed: 'it would in my judgement be madness to place such confidence in that supply'. The journey to India from Norfolk Island was too long and inconvenient, and would make the goods expensive. Continued shipments from Europe would make such an enterprise precarious from the settlers' point of view. Vessels in the India country trade already used perfectly satisfactory substitutes for European maritime stores: gummatty and coir made good cables and running rigging, and masts could be procured much closer to hand in Sumatra and Borneo. In summary, he said

The absurdity of such an idea, as bringing so bulky an article as Hemp and Cordage for our Marine Yards from so great a distance and consequently at so high a freight, is too great to merit any serious consideration; tho' the introduction of the New Zealand Hemp Plant into Britain is an object of great National Importance, and as such worthy the Company's attention.

It is interesting that the only offical references to the production of New Zealand flax, other than in the 'Heads of a Plan', were to its being produced in England from imported plant or seed specimens.[30]

Having disposed of the flax and masts idea, Dalrymple went on to demolish the other aspects of Young's and Call's proposal:

This project of a Settlement in that quarter has appeared in many Proteus-like forms, sometimes as a halfway house to China; again as a check upon the *Spaniards* at *Manila* and their *Acapulco* Trade; sometimes as a place for transported Convicts; then as a place of Asylum for American Refugees;

and sometimes as an Emporium for supplying our Marine yards with Hemp and Cordage, or for carrying on the Fur Trade on the N.W. Coast of America; just as the temper of ministers was supposed to be inclined to receive a favorable impression.

Dalrymple captured neatly the cynical nature of these proposals. He denied that a more expeditious passage to China could be found via Norfolk Island. 'This opinion was the offspring of ignorance supposing those parts where no Lands were described to be open Sea because unknown.' He argued that the distance was much greater than by the conventional routes, and sailing time would be extended because of the unreliable winds and the danger of uncharted seas.

Admitting Dalrymple's prejudice as an employee of the East India Company, he nevertheless distilled the essential character of Matra, Young and Call's schemes very well. They were visionary, extravagant, even Utopian. Their shape changed according to the requirements of the government. Their ultimate function was to secure employment or opportunity for the promoters. The Pitt ministry took them all with a grain of salt, and was only interested in them in the context of the convict problem.

In the autumn of 1785 the ministry received another plan for the disposal of convicts. Yet again the penal element was a secondary component of the plan. The site in question was the 'Caffre Coast', just west of present day Port Elizabeth in South Africa. Here, as with the Das Voltas Bay plan, Pitt and his colleagues tinkered with the suggestion of combining a naval station and place of refreshment with a convict colony. After all, both sites were on the sea route to India. The strongest recommendation of the Caffre Coast scheme came indirectly from Colonel William Dalrymple, an East India Company employee whose ship had been forced to take refuge at this spot in May. The proposal was sent originally to William Devaynes, the Chairman of the Company, who forwarded it to Henry Dundas and Pitt in September. Dalrymple saw a settlement there as having great advantages in wartime:

We have lost America, and a half way House wou'd secure us India, and an Empire to Britain—We are at a loss where to send our Convicts—to send them to this Country wou'd indeed be a Paradise to them, and Settlers wou'd crowd there.[31]

It is not clear that Pitt was actually looking for a paradise for convicts. Dalrymple, of course, was looking for the command of an expedition to this area, and he had the support of Devaynes. Pitt sought the opinions of his colleagues, but the matter was eventually left to rest. Presumably, as Frost has argued, this was because the Das Voltas survey was already underway.[32] However the main objection was obviously that the area was already settled by Dutch farmers. Given the delicacy of the diplomatic situation in Europe in

1785 and 1786, the British were most reluctant to arouse the hostility of the Netherlands.

When the ship *Nautilus* returned from the south Atlantic with its unfavourable report on the Das Voltas Bay area, more plans for the disposal of convicts appeared. Some of these were reviewed by government. It was presumably at this time that the Home Office reconsidered the costs of transportation to New South Wales, assessed Sir Watkin Lewes' proposal to employ 600 convicts from the hulks in the Woolwich Rope Yards, and considered the plan for employing the same number in the Scottish coal mines. At the same time John Call's scheme for New South Wales was re-examined. These plans appear in that order in the Home Office papers covering the period May to August 1786. The only element common to them all, and the one which clearly interested the government, was their potential capacity to solve the convict problem.

In these vital months of decision about transportation another voice was added to the debate. Captain John Blankett had shown a long-standing interest in the defence of the sea passage to India, and during the American War of Independence he had been one of those urging the government to attack the Dutch at the Cape of Good Hope. On hearing of the fruitless *Nautilus* expedition, Blankett suggested Tristan da Cunha or Madagascar as suitable alternatives.[33] Both these sites would be cheap to establish and maintain, and Blankett correctly assumed that cost was a major consideration with the ministry. Both places were adjacent to the sea routes to or from India and opened up prospects of commercial development.

Frost makes much of Blankett's letter to Nepean a few days later on the subject of Madagascar, in which he asserted that 'he had reason to think that if it becomes a Naval question that Idea will be adopted'.[34] Frost takes this as strong proof that the government invariably linked the disposal of convicts with naval strategy. Such an interpretation totally ignores the qualification 'if' in Blankett's letter. It ignores the fact that Madagascar was directly on the two most regular sailing routes to Bombay, Madras and the Persian Gulf, which passed either side of it. It ignores the fact that at least one member of the ministry was sceptical of Blankett's scheme, and it was in any case never adopted. To transpose the supposed advantages of Das Voltas Bay, or Madagascar—both on the sea routes to India —to Botany Bay, many thousands of miles from those routes, is a geographical absurdity, and the Pitt ministry certainly was not party to it.[35]

After the August decision to send convicts to Botany Bay, suggestions for other sites continued to reach the government. On 1 September Alexander Dalrymple recommended again Tristan da Cunha, which he had first nominated for settlement some fifteen years before. This island would be an inexpensive alternative to New South Wales, and would be more likely to offer possibilities for the reform of convicts.[36] Two months later Captain Blankett brought forward the Madagascar plan again, without substantial modification.[37] By the end of that year, however, it had become apparent that the government had fixed firmly the destination of the first fleet, and the tendering of other potential sites declined.

In later years the same selection of sites were brought up again, either for commercial reasons, or as possible penal settlements. In the early years of New South Wales, when it was at its most precarious, the possibility of founding additional convict colonies was kept alive. The ministry was totally unaware of the potential capacity of what was initially intended to be a purely penal colony, and perhaps hoped that a site incurring lower transport costs might be found. Early commercial interest in New South Wales was tentative, to say the least, and came principally from groups such as the whalers, who were interested in New South Wales as a possible base for refitting and refreshment. In May 1788, before any information had come back from New South Wales, Young and Call resurrected their 1785 plan for a settlement on Norfolk Island, to supply naval stores to India. At this stage they seemed completely unaware that orders had been given to Governor Phillip to establish an outpost on the island, and they asked that it be granted to them and their heirs in perpetuity. This proposal was ignored by the ministry, and is important only in so far as it revealed where the true interests of Young and Call lay.[38]

At the time that the ministry was reviewing the need for a survey of the south Atlantic in 1789, Captain Blankett was consulted on the possible value of Tristan da Cunha. While pointing to its location astride the sea routes to India, and its potential as a convict colony, he was reticent about speculating on its other possible uses:

Of Probable advantages I have forebore to speak as it might have the appearance of being too sanguine & intended only to propose a Job for myself.[39]

In the context of other great planners of his time, this was indeed modest of him. Blankett was the most well-informed of the private individuals who drafted proposals for the southern oceans after 1783, and with Sir Joseph Banks, was the only one whose opinions were regarded as reliable. The irony in Blankett's reference to a job, hints that the ministry viewed other proposals as self-interested and self-promoting. Admiral Young's lament in 1793, that he had never been consulted about the founding of Botany Bay, could well have been echoed by others:

I must say that had I been honor'd with but a single conference on the subject of my own plan, I should most certainly have proposed a constant supply of provisions &c for the convicts, from the Island of Madagascar.[40]

There is no evidence that Matra, Call or Young were in fact consulted directly by government after their evidence before the Beauchamp Committee. Indeed in Young's case, there is conclusive evidence that he was ignored. His association with Call suggests that neither had anything to do with the final decision on Botany Bay.

It is therefore highly misleading to draw any conclusions about government intentions from the private plans of these private individuals. Nevertheless a number of the historians of the founding of Botany Bay have drawn on these schemes in just this way. In the cases of Matra, Call, Young and William Dalrymple, employment or commercial gain, or both provided the inspiration for their proposals. Both Young and Call were fickle about their attachment to particular sites, and saw the supposed advantages as readily movable from one to another, almost irrespective of location and climate. Most of the proposals began as recommendations for settlement, and were only subsequently modified to deal with the convict problem. After the founding of the New South Wales colony Young and Call returned to their original commercial scheme. By 1786 Matra had taken advantage of Banks's patronage to obtain a consular position at Tangiers. He was therefore no longer interested in either convicts, Loyalists or New South Wales. That the Pitt ministry referred at all to the proposals of these men can be taken as a measure of its desperation, rather than as recognition of their strategic or commercial merits. In fact the ministry totally ignored such references, and was solely interested in potential convict colonies.

These rather romantic and impractical schemes have had a much greater impact on historians than they had on the ministry of William Pitt. They have diverted the debate on the origins of New South Wales into speculative channels about commerce, naval stores and strategy, and away from the central issue of an overwhelming penal problem. By following the government search for a site for a penal colony, it is possible to see how marginal to the discussions the private plans were.

Chapter 4

GOVERNMENT PLANS FOR THE DISPOSAL OF CONVICTS

In spite of the growing power of the movements for penal reform, successive British governments after 1775 did not consider seriously the alternatives to transportation. As has already been explained, there were good political, financial and ideological reasons for their attitude. In the early stages of the American War there was every reason to believe that the conflict would be short-lived, and before long convicts would again be dumped in Maryland and Virginia. In the meantime the hulks would hold them as a 'temporary expedient'. When England's fortunes in the war deteriorated, such a prospect looked less and less likely, and although the American alternative was not finally abandoned until 1786, consideration had to be given to alternative possibilities.

At first sight other British trans-Atlantic colonies seemed to provide the most promising opportunities. However, opposition to transportation had appeared in all the American colonies before 1775, and was particularly vociferous in the West Indies.[1] Planters who were becoming increasingly concerned about the restiveness of slaves did not want their public order problems increased by an inflow of felons as plantation labour. For this reason most of the colonial assemblies had passed laws to keep convicts out, and although these were subject to imperial review, the planters' arguments and determination were difficult to ignore.[2] Attempts to do so at Honduras, and Barbuda in the Leeward Islands, met with disaster in the 1780s.

Canada, Nova Scotia and Newfoundland offered no more promise, although the Pitt ministry did not rule out the last two entirely until the 1790s. These northern colonies were not suitable for indentured labour on the same basis as the former southern plantation colonies, because the nature of their economies was not amenable to it. There was supposedly no permanent settlement in Newfoundland in peace time, and certainly very little productive work for convicts to do there. The contractor Duncan Campbell testified

before the House of Commons in 1779 that none of the remaining
British North American colonies were suitable for transportation
on the old system, a view supported by Undersecretary of State
Evan Nepean before the Beauchamp Committee in 1785.[3]

The Parliamentary debates on the annual review of the Hulks
Act always produced a crop of suggestions of possible sites for transportation, including Canada, Nova Scotia, the West and East Indies,
Africa, New Zealand and even the Falkland Islands.[4] However,
many of these alternatives involved a departure from the usual
eighteenth- century pattern of transportation in the form of indentured labour, to one necessitating a guard system and extensive
victualling and clothing costs. Financially and administratively this
was unattractive, and in many contexts simply not feasible. After
all, to use convicts to found a strategic base was at least as expensive
as using regular troops, and much more troublesome since the convicts themselves required a guard and would present security problems.

There was no established tradition in England of using convicts
to found bases or commercial entrepôts, and any such innovation
would have been a radical departure from existing practice, and a
likely disaster. For the governments facing the penal problem after
1775, such alternatives would always be a last resort, and this explained the continued attachment to North American sites long
after the option seemed closed.

The Committee reviewing the Hulks Act in 1779, meeting after
the disaster of Saratoga, widened its brief to consider alternative
transportation sites to North American ones.[5] Botany Bay, Gibral-
tar, the Gambia and Senegal were put forward by various interested
individuals, and this Committee thus recognized the possibility of
a departure from the normal indenture system. Nevertheless an
attempt was made to lay down the criteria for a penal colony, with
the emphasis on avoiding cost. Thus, the site had to have fertile soil
so that convicts would be self-sufficient agriculturalists after one
year, 'with little or no Aid from the Mother Country'. It was also
necessary that the settlement be distant and isolated so that escape
would be difficult. The ideal location was therefore a place where
convicts could be dumped and more or less left to themselves with
a minimal guard. Although this would lower the establishment costs,
it was also rather unrealistic. Nevertheless, these requirements for
a penal colony were adhered to, and later defined more precisely
by the Beauchamp Committee.

It was to the 1779 Committee on Transportation—the Bunbury
Committee as it became known—that Sir Joseph Banks gave his
well known testimony in favour of New South Wales. For the most
part he depended on his recollections from the *Endeavour* voyage,
and these were not infallible. Was the abundance of timber which
he remembered suitable for building purposes, or just firewood?

Was his belief that convicts would be able to maintain themselves after a year a realistic one?[6] Banks seemed to be referring to his journal records, but conflated his opinions of Botany Bay with those on the continent as a whole.

The Committee concluded that while 'atrocious' criminals might be sent to work in unhealthy climates where their lives might be at risk, young convicts might best be disposed of in 'some distant Part of the Globe, and in new-discovered Countries where the Climate is healthy, and the Means of Support attainable'.[7] Such alternatives could not be pursued without changes to the legislation, which permitted sentences of transportation only to America. The appropriate legislation allowing the substitution of other destinations was passed the same year. One neglected section of this Act also provided for the establishment of penitentiaries.

In the closing stages of the American War the North and Shelburne administrations tried the experiment of using convicts as part of a military force defending African forts. Little is known about the second of these experiments, but from the Beauchamp Committee minutes it is clear that the first was a disaster. Between 200 and 350 convicts were taken to Cape Coast Castle under military discipline. Between twenty and thirty died on the voyage out. The provisions were found to be grossly inadequate, and riots broke out shortly after the party landed at the fort. A group of convicts captured a Portuguese ship, and others deserted to the Dutch. The remainder either succumbed to disease or were shipped home.[8]

This experience rather dampened enthusiasm for using large numbers of convicts in a strategic or military role in such bases. The problems of supervision made their defence role pointless. The second batch of convicts were therefore shipped out purely as transportees, although without any more coherent planning. 'The grand consideration seems to be, to get them out of Europe at all Events', wrote the despondent Governor of Cape Coast Castle in February 1783.[9]

Further obstacles in 1783 and 1784 highlighted the difficulties of breaking from a past pattern of transportation without incurring considerable expense. In the middle of 1783 the Home Secretary, Lord North, contracted with a shipper named George Moore to carry 143 convicts to North America at a cost of £3 per head. This suggests the felons were to be indentured at the end of their voyage. There is some confusion over the exact destination of these men. Court records imply that the original plan may have been to take them to Virginia or Maryland, but that the contractor was determined to dump them at the first site available.[10] He later testified that they were to go to Nova Scotia, and the official records suggest that this was the true destination.

Whatever the intention, this expedition ended in chaos. Just off the Downs in August, a mutiny broke out on board the poorly guarded ship and forty-eight of the convicts on board made their escape by landing on the Sussex coast to the east of Rye. They were eventually taken into custody and subsequently appeared at the Old Bailey on charges of being at large in the Kingdom having returned from transportation. Eight of them were hanged. It is doubtful whether the outcome would have have been more successful had the trans-Atlantic voyage been completed, given the attitude of the Nova Scotians to accepting convicts.[11]

In the following April there was a similar mutiny aboard the vessel *Mercury* in Torbay. The original destination of this shipment was again to be Nova Scotia, although a deliberate cloak of obscurity was drawn over the whole matter. Giving evidence at a trial after the mutiny, a steward from the ship testified that she was to sail first to Baltimore, then to Honduras, then to Virginia and thence to Nova Scotia.[12] Before this rather suspicious route could be pursued, the ninety convicts on board the *Mercury* overpowered the guards and took to the boats. Most of the convicts were apprehended by the crew of a naval vessel before they could make the shore, but twenty-four managed to land and make for freedom. All those still at large were eventually recaptured and tried at the Exeter Assizes in May. The remainder, having been retaken at sea, could not be tried for 'being at large in the Kingdom' and were simply returned to the *Mercury* in chains.

When most of the convicts were back on the *Mercury* she sailed for the United States. Unable to unload her cargo there, she sailed on to Honduras. Here the felons were landed and work on a settlement begun. Local British logwood cutters then put an end to the enterprise, placing a 'ban' on the indenture of the convicts and beginning court proceedings against the shipowner's agents.[13] The experiment therefore ended in chaos, as did another in the following year in which Moore was involved. Nepean later testified to the Beauchamp Committee that Moore's 1784 voyage had been undertaken without government authorization.[14]

It is likely that Nepean was being wise after the event, for there were good diplomatic reasons for establishing a more secure British presence in Honduras after the war. That region had been one of the bones of contention in the peace negotiations with Spain, and Britain had to fight for a real presence there. The Spaniards had wanted to keep Britain out, and to supply logwood to British ships without permitting them to land or to cut wood. There was a good argument therefore for Britain firmly staking its claim.[15] Regardless of the actual events, the three attempts by George Moore to carry convicts to North America had failed. It is clear they were ill-conceived and badly organized. Two mutinies out of three voyages suggests the vessels were under-manned and ill-secured. The governments had been forced to rather desperate measures in attempting to keep expenses low in the context of the traditional indenture system of transportation. But the alternatives available to them were few, short of using compulsion to force convicts on unwilling colonies. Lord Sydney made this point in the context of the Honduras fiasco: 'The more I consider the matter the greater difficulty I see in disposing of these people in any other place in the possession [sic] His Majesty's Subjects.'[16]

There was one last effort to dispose of convicts without incurring great expense. In October Evan Nepean approached the Portuguese Consul to see if convicts might be sent to their colonies. When this was referred to Lisbon, the Queen declined the offer of British felons and another avenue was closed.[17]

In the second half of 1784 the Pitt ministry shifted its priorities concerning transportation sites. It began to consider proposals for guarded colonies in regions where there was no possibility of supplying indentured labour. In December the government began searching for sites by a process of elimination. It revealed proposals for Botany Bay, Bencoolen, Sumatra and Cape Coast Castle. In the course of its review it looked once more at the testimonies from Banks and Matra on Botany Bay, Governor Roberts on Cape Coast Castle, and a Mr Herbert and Mr Wyatt on Bencoolen and Sumatra. The last two were soon ruled out, even though they might be considered to have the sort of strategic value to which historians such as Frost have referred.[18]

In an atmosphere of increasing panic and political pressure over the convict predicament, more extensive consideration was given to the options of Botany Bay and West Africa. To deal with acute local problems Lord Sydney was obliged to resort to short term and *ad hoc* solutions. In mid-December he asked the Africa Committee if twenty convicts could be taken out and distributed among the African forts, a proposal which was accepted by the Committee Chairman.[19]

Such expedients did not help to resolve the general crisis. In the same month the Cabinet and Home Department officials addressed themselves to the entire problem, with the focus on New South Wales and West Africa. From the outset of these discussions it was clear that a West African site was preferred. New South Wales met some of the criteria, being unsettled by Europeans, relatively underpopulated by the Aborigines, and capable of growing European foods and raising European stock. As a guarded site it would also meet the second most vital need: in the cryptic words of a Home Office clerk, 'Not easy to escape—they are far distant from Europeans'.[20]

In two linked respects, however, New South Wales was not favourably regarded by the Pitt ministry. It was not only distant, it was *too* distant; therefore it was a costly alternative. The two principal proposals for transportation were circulated amongst the ministry in the weeks around Christmas 1784. The general conclusions were embodied in the verdict of the First Lord of the Admiralty on Matra's proposal: the length of the voyage to Botany Bay, which Banks had calculated at approximately seven months, made the site impractical as a place of regular resort.[21] In the view of the Cabinet no countervailing advantages were produced to offset this factor.

The historian Frost has assumed that the government thought of New South Wales in strategic terms because of the appearance of two other plans relating to the defence of India among the cabinet papers of 25 and 26 December 1784. That assumption is unwarranted and unproven, based on an as yet 'unrecovered' letter from Pitt to Howe, the contents of which Frost guesses at.[22] One cannot draw historical conclusions from the often accidental appearance of papers adjacent to one another in Home Office files. Nothing in the consideration of Matra's, Lacam's and the East India Company proposals for the Nicobars and Acheen suggests that these proposals are related to New South Wales. In their reference to possible convict sites in December 1784, the Cabinet and Home Office officials did not raise the questions of strategy and commerce but restricted themselves to the problem at hand.

Even while the Cabinet was considering various alternatives in December, it was clear that Lord Sydney's preference (and that of Nepean, his Undersecretary of State) lay with an African site. On 29 December Nepean revealed the ministry's intention to the Mayor of Plymouth:

It is at last determined that they shall forthwith be removed, with some others who are now in the Gaols in and about London, to the coast of Africa . . . which you know in the routine of Punishment is considered as next in degree to that of Death.[23]

He enjoined the mayor to secrecy 'for it would be likely to create trouble were the intentions of government known with respect to the destination of the Convicts'. As Gillen has pointed out, it was this fear of a public and Parliamentary reaction which shaped the government's behaviour over the next few months. Nevertheless, by the new year the Cabinet was energetic in giving the African plan practical shape.

It is tempting to see another significant aspect to the government's preference for a West African site. During the peace negotiations of 1783 it became clear that France was determined to regain much of the ground in West Africa which it had lost in 1763. In particular it was interested in the Senegal and the region embracing the gum trade between the Gambia and Arguin. As a result of the peace settlement, the former Crown Colony of Senegambia was split. Senegal and its dependent factories were transferred to France but the gum trade was rather vaguely guaranteed to both nations, with rights of access up the Gambia itself. Britain was guaranteed the possession of James Island and the Gambia.[24]

Since a great part of the former Crown Colony was cut off in this way by the treaty, the British government decided to rest control of the Gambia in the less than enthusiastic hands of the Company of Merchants Trading to Africa, which had administered the forts before 1756. This body was badly organized and virtually moribund by 1783, and was understandably reluctant to devote much energy to administering an area which might be removed from its control at any time. Immediately after the peace settlement the French took the opportunity to establish firmly their presence in the area, and to exploit the ambiguity and loopholes in the treaty. Trading vessels were despatched to the Gambia in 1783. To those manning and patrolling the British Gambia forts it seemed that the French were exploiting the situation in order to take control of the gum trade. To make matters worse, the forts in the region were dilapidated and undermanned, and requests to the government for financial assistance in upgrading them were ignored.[25]

There were pressures on the government to take a tougher line with the French and to strengthen the British military presence on the Gambia. One of the regular visitors to the forts was Captain Edward Thompson, who had been routinely involved in the inspection of stations, and in naval patrols in West African waters. In the course of 1784 and early 1785 he pointed out on a number of occasions to the Lords of the Admiralty the weakness of the forts and the need for reinforcement.[26]

In this context it would therefore be tempting to view the Cabinet's decision to settle convicts up the Gambia as central to a strategic and commercial plan for the region. However there are considerable difficulties with such an analysis. First, and in spite of alarms such as those raised by Thompson, government interest in the Gambia was lukewarm and there is no evidence of a willingness to strengthen the military presence in the region. The decision to pass the administration of the area back to the Africa Committee was a sign that the government at the time believed that the Gambia was more trouble than it was worth. Second, no mention was made of strategic or commercial motives when the convict possibilities were being investigated. The disposal of convicts appeared to be the only object of contemplation. Third, convicts would be very doubtful assets from a strategic point of view, and the experience of 1782 highlighted this aspect. Other than staking a claim, a convict colony was more likely to be a strategic liability, as was the case with New South Wales after 1788. Finally, the actual site selected by the government was so distant from the coast that it would have been of no military value whatsoever.

Suggestions for convict colonies on the Gambia had been put forward in 1776 by the Deputy-Governor of James Island, and in again in 1779 by John Roberts, a former Governor of Cape Coast Castle.[27] Although Cape Coast Castle had itself been suggested, there was resistance to stationing convicts in any number at active trading posts and it was for this reason that attention focused on the Gambia. Eventually the choice was narrowed to the island of Lemain. This is present day MacCarthy Island, the site of the city of Georgetown, about 250 kilometres towards the head of the river. The suggestion for this site was put forward by John Barnes, the Governor of the Africa Company, and by the middle of January an emissary had been sent out to survey the island and arrange for its purchase.[28] There was some doubt about the qualifications of the man sent out on this delicate mission, Richard Bradley. Although he left England with the expectation of having the eventual direction of the convict enterprise, by February the government had other plans. Once in the Gambia, Bradley found difficulties in dealing with the local chiefs and the negotiations became protracted and expensive.[29]

The plans went ahead a little more smoothly in England—in the beginning. Responsibility for the planning was in the capable hands of the Undersecretary of State, Evan Nepean. He dealt with the Africa Committee, gathered in reports on the Gambia and its inhabitants, sought quotations from contractors and attempted to estimate the cost of the whole operation. By the end of January 1785 Nepean had also found a suitable director for the convict colony: John Heatley, a man with some knowledge of the Gambia and contacts among the local population.

With the ground work supposedly done, Sydney sent out the appropriate orders to the Treasury on 9 February for the establishment of a convict settlement on the island of Lemain. The objective was to get the transportees established before the beginning of the rainy season in June, when the river was at its most unhealthy and oppressive. There was apparently no intention to await a favourable report from Bradley. Indeed, indecent haste was evident at each stage of the plan. The information gathered on Lemain was vague, speculative and often erroneous—it was even stated to be three times further up the Gambia than it actually was.[30]

The preface to the order of 9 February was in the same form as the later orders for Botany Bay, and referred in the same terms to overcrowded jails and the likelihood of disease. Initially, the plan called for the removal to Lemain of only 150 convicts, amounting to one shipload. They would be landed with six months' provisions and some goods for trading purposes. To prevent the convicts from escaping or moving downstream to interfere with regular trade, a brigantine or schooner of about 120 tons would be stationed in the river as a guardship. Although this was to be a private vessel supplied and manned by the contractor, it would be subject to checks during the routine naval inspection of African forts.

Accompanying this order was a general paper on Lemain based on the opinions of members of the Africa Committee. In every way this document was the equivalent of the later 'Heads of a Plan'. The document gave an optimistic account of the island and its capacity to sustain a convict population. The island was described as fertile and able to produce crops within four months of a landing. The merchants believed the convicts could be left to their own devices to govern themselves, apart from the guardship in the river. There would be nowhere for them to escape to, and left to themselves they would soon become planters of tobacco, cotton, indigo and yams. It was inevitable in the first year that 'a great many of the Convicts would die from the change of Climate', but as the settlement became more stable and more convicts were sent out, the food supply would improve, and the island would eventually be able to accommodate 4000 transportees. Eventually they would form their own government, grow rich and therefore honest, and many would return home as reformed characters. Arcady would therefore purify just as the old society had corrupted. As Gillen has pointed out, this vision was so naive in its assumptions that it would be unwise to assume that the Pitt ministry paid much attention to it.[31]

The ministry certainly would have paid attention to the projected financing of the operation, which was enclosed with the draft scheme. The cost of disposing of the first 500 convicts was calculated to be no more than £20 per head, including shipping, clothing, provisioning, implements and trading goods. This was about the same as the cost of maintaining convicts in the Thames hulks, and it would tend to fall as the community grew and became self-sufficient in food. With this estimate were enclosed also the proposal of the contractor, Anthony Calvert, the details of the armed ship, and Heatley's terms for accepting the position as agent of the government.

It was apparent that the government's main concern was to dispose of a substantial portion of the jail population as soon as conveniently possible and even at the risk of considerable loss of life.

The probability of loss of life had been raised by the merchants, and the experience with troops in West Africa, together with the convict experiment of 1782 must have been known to the ministry. In his evidence before the Beauchamp Committee in April 1785, Evan Nepean adopted a rather cavalier attitude to this aspect, and saw it as no barrier to the Lemain plan. By the end of February the jail situation was such that the government was contemplating increasing the first shipload of convicts to 200, but by this time it was uncertain whether the expedition could be got underway in order to arrive in the Gambia before the rainy season began.[33]

By this time the government found itself on the horns of a dilemma. The Transportation Act, *24 Geo. III c.12.*, was due for renewal, and the whole question of the disposal of convicts in this context would be raised as an issue in the Commons. Even excepting the lateness of the season it seemed unlikely that the convicts could be shipped out to West Africa before the Act expired. In addition, the government was experiencing difficulty with the contractors. When Calvert's proposal for the shipping was submitted to the Navy Board, its members argued that it was too high, and they were unhappy also with the terms on which John Barnes offered to supply the guardship.[34] By early March the ministry had recognized that the time for shipping in the current season had passed, and the plan was shelved until the autumn. Nevertheless the government was determined to push the House of Commons into accepting a West African site.[35]

The Committee which convened in April 1785 to consider the question of transportation met in an atmosphere of growing hostility to the notion of sending convicts to die up the Gambia. In spite of the ministry's attempts to keep the proposal secret, it was inevitable that information would leak out. By March, awkward questions were being asked in the Commons by men such as Burke and Beauchamp on the opposition benches.[36] It was in the face of attacks from these quarters that Pitt conceded to an appraisal by a Committee. The Committee was to be chaired by Lord Beauchamp, and its broad membership included Burke, Fox, William Eden, Lord Mulgrave and the ubiquitous John Call.

The Committee proceeded by briefly examining evidence on the condition of the jails, scrutinizing the Gambia proposal and then taking evidence on other possible sites for transportation. The information on the condition of the jails was based on testimony about Lancaster and Newgate: one the most dismal of prisons, and the other the most populous. Since the penal problem was well understood generally, little time was spent on background information, and the Committee quickly turned its attention to government plans to deal with the problem.

On 27 April Nepean gave evidence before the Committee in favour of the Lemain scheme. It was not an impressive performance. He referred to the problems of the jails and the hulks and then sketched out the Lemain proposal, assuring the Committee that it had not received final approval, but was 'preferred to every other Plan'. The destructive effects of the climate and disease were hinted at in his admission that only 200 of the most notorious and dangerous felons—'the worst of both sexes'—would be sent, and that as the costings were based on the survival of them all, the estimates were on the generous side. In justifying the choice, he listed the sites which had proved impossible: Honduras, Cape Breton, Nova Scotia and Canada. In these places there had been strong local resistance. In answering a question as to whether the island of Lemain was ready for their reception, he conceded that sovereignty had not been transferred. However, the government expected soon to be in possession of the island. By its own admission, the government had therefore shown the Lemain scheme to have been hastily conceived, poorly planned and even callous.[37]

Although John Barnes supported the proposal on behalf of the Africa Committee, a string of later witnesses with experience of the Gambia, demolished the idea thoroughly. Mr Boone, an army surgeon, Sir John Call, Sir George Young, Captain Edward Thompson, Mr Henry Smeathman, a Mr Sturt and a captain in the African trade all pointed to the devastating effects of climate and disease. The mortality among the convicts would probably be extremely high. Some witnesses believed the local populations were of uncertain temperament, and even likely to attack the convicts. Commodore Thompson and the trading captain, John Nevan, asserted that one guardship would not contain the convicts and that the presence of the convicts would damage the trade in the region. When the Beauchamp Committee presented its first interim report to the House on 9 May, the Lemain plan was no longer considered although poor Bradley was still up the Gambia treating for territory.[38]

The government was bereft of a solution to the penal problem and contrary to the views of some historians, it seemed to be taking its lead from the Committee.[39] Sydney admitted to members of the Committee that no obvious alternative existed in the Home Office files, stating 'that different Ideas had been suggested on the Subject, but that such Suggestions were either made in Conversation, or appeared from the Nature of them, unworthy the attention of the Committee, and that no such plan as was required existed in his office'.[40] Sydney stated the situation much more bluntly to Sir John Wrottesley:

. . . from the mistaken humanity of some and the affected tenderness of others, every Plan, which the King's servants have proposed for transporting the convicts out of the Kingdom, has met with such opposition, that it has been almost impossible to carry any of them into Execution.[41]

The administration did not act decisively 'to turn affairs in their favour', but drifted helplessly as the Committee followed its own course.

The Committee turned its attention to New South Wales, taking evidence from Matra, Sir Joseph Banks and the contractor Duncan Campbell. The evidence of both Matra and Banks was predictable. Matra suggested that any number of settlements might be established along the New South Wales coast, incorporating convict and non-convict populations. For a penal settlement an initial shipment of 500 convicts with 200 soldiers and a guardship would be appropriate. This contingent should leave England in August, procuring supplies at the Cape on the way. It is not obvious why he thought the convicts should reach their destination at the beginning of winter. Women could be gathered from the Pacific Islands in order to keep the convicts happy and docile. He did not see that there needed to be any further examination of New South Wales. Matra indicated also his eagerness to command the settlement.[42] Banks gave his opinion the following day, 10 May, and in his evidence were echoes of his testimony of 1779 before the Bunbury Committee. He directed his comments primarily towards the Botany Bay region, and his views were a little more qualified than those of Matra. While assuring the Committee that the area would be suitable for 500 convicts, he hinted at problems with building materials and the water supply. The soil was swampy in parts, or a light sand mould, suitable for cattle grazing and low intensity cultivation. While not ideal for a settlement it would be adequate for a penal colony.

At this point in the discussions New South Wales was emerging as an alternative site presenting only minor problems. It is interesting to note that throughout the questioning of the witnesses, only the convict requirement was referred to: there were no references to the strategic or commercial benefits likely to accrue from such a settlement. However, on 12 May, crucial evidence was given to the Committee which led to the temporary shelving of the New South Wales option.

Neither Matra nor Banks had provided information on the costs of shipping convicts to New South Wales or maintaining them there; neither was in a particularly good position to do so. On 12 May the Committee sought such information from the East India Company, and from Duncan Campbell, the contractor involved in transportation to the American colonies before 1775. The evidence of Coggan, the East India Company clerk, related to the expenses of shipping men to India. Without food and medical expenses this came to £25 a man. Duncan Campbell's evidence confirmed the Committee's worst fears. If 500 convicts could be crammed into a 700 to 800 ton vessel the costs of shipping them and chartering the ship for a round trip would not be less than £30 per man. If the ship carried only 200 convicts the cost would rise to £40. This did not include provisions for the first months in New South Wales, tools and implements needed for cultivation, building materials or additional clothing and blankets. The total cost would be close to twice that of maintaining convicts in the hulks or sending them to the island of Lemain.[43] Eight months later Campbell was to produce an even gloomier estimate for establishing a settlement, which took the cost for 270 convicts and a marine guard to £50.8.2d.[44]

Although Matra was recalled by the Committee eleven days later to give his opinions on the cost and method of supplying New South Wales, and to comment on Campbell's calculations, it was obvious that the Committee had all but abandoned the idea of the site. They promptly turned their attention to Das Voltas Bay in present-day Namibia.

The reason for the Committee's change of focus was not strategic or commercial, but financial. From the accession of the Pitt ministry there were two overriding considerations in seeking a solution to the convict problem. One was the great urgency of the matter, as explained in this and preceding chapters. The other was cost. On this second question the ministry and especially its leader were particularly sensitive. Economy was a principal concern of the landed class in the eighteenth century and the spiralling cost of the American War had focused their attention more sharply upon it. The belief that government had either knowingly or unknowingly permitted expenditure to go unchecked informed the opposition to Lord North and provided the impetus behind the Economical Reform movement. William Pitt's first speech in the House in February 1781 was on the subject of Economical Reform, and his second, two months later, was on the Commission on Public Accounts.[45] During his Parliamentary career one of Pitt's greatest concerns was to reduce government expenditure, and it was the area of some of his most significant successes. When the impetus for Parliamentary Reform ebbed in the mid-1780s, he diverted his efforts into financial and administrative reform, carrying over his commitment to economical government. The attempts to reduce the National Debt—which had increased threefold in thirty years—were applauded by the country gentlemen, as were the efforts to reduce the routine costs of government offices.[46]

Pitt's concern for financial reform was a personal commitment, but also a political necessity. In the conditions of political flux after 1783 Pitt was never able to be sure of his Parliamentary majorities. Although the Whigs were often dispirited and divided, they defeated the government on the Westminster scrutiny and the initial proposals of the Duke of Richmond to fortify the Portsmouth and Plymouth dockyards. On this latter issue two of the independent country members vitally interested in the convict problem voted against the government.[47] Pitt's favourite measure, Parliamentary Reform, was defeated in 1785, as were his Irish Commercial proposals. In fact, on the same day that Duncan Campbell was giving his gloomy estimates of the cost of transportation to New South Wales, Pitt's reintroduced Irish Commercial Bill was viciously lampooned in the House by Fox and was headed for defeat.[48] The lesson to be learned from these defeats was that the independent country members were still vital to the survival of the ministry. Should the government find itself out on a political limb the independents would not hesitate to saw it off. With its financial implications, and its connection to local government, the convict problem offered just such an opportunity.

By the time of the Beauchamp Committee hearings, the debate on the renewal of transportation had been thoroughly engaged and the cost of each proposal was a matter of critical concern. If the charge for the traditional means of disposing of felons—transportation—rose substantially above other options, the government would be in a vulnerable position. The acceptable premium for housing the convicts further from Westminster than the hulks was vaguely stated, but keenly felt. Financial concern accounted for the frequent requests for estimates both before and after the decision for Botany Bay. The greatest objections to proposals such as those of Matra, Call, Young and Banks therefore were financial ones, and the various strategic, commercial and communication applications attached to New South Wales were too visionary to offer any prospect of offsetting the cost of transporting and maintaining convicts. For the promoters of such schemes the cost disadvantage had to be counterbalanced by other positive advantages, and some proponents overreached themselves in fictionalizing the virtues of New South Wales. Those virtues were paraded and praised at length before the Beauchamp Committee, and it is evident that proposals for New South Wales took up much of the Committee's time. From the government's point of view, once forced into the corner which became New South Wales, the sole value of those ulterior advantages of the site was as a smokescreen.

For the Pitt government the only moderating factor on the issue of cost was the degree of urgency operating on the convict problem. This aspect has been considered in detail in Chapter 2, and it is clear that by 1784 there was a severe convict problem. Stop-gap measure such as the hulks failed to contain the crisis and generated difficulties of their own. By rejecting the Gambia option the Beauchamp Committee impeded progress, and by forcing a survey of Das Voltas Bay it delayed a solution to the convict problem for another year at least. The parlous situation in the jails and hulks was, in turn, exacerbated. By May 1786 Pitt was so pressed on this issue that he gave assurances about the immediate resumption of transportation before the results of the Das Voltas survey were known. When that survey proved negative the government found itself in an invidious position. For the first time the overriding concern of cost was replaced with the political one of urgency. The ministry plumped for New South Wales.

However the cost factor soon re-asserted itself, and with added importance. From the moment the decision was announced (and attacks on it began) the planners of the first fleet, and its commander, were enjoined to economy. Everything was done to reduce the cost of the enterprise. The stores were cheap and shoddy. The equipment level was low, in spite of Governor Phillip's good efforts. The rations for the marines were below the level normally issued. The size of the garrison was dangerously small. As one of the major expenses was to be the upkeep and manning of the naval vessel on station, it was proposed that the warship *Sirius* should be withdrawn from New South Wales once the settlement was established. Her tender was the smallest and cheapest ship that could be of any use to the colony. Economic considerations continued to predominate in the early years of the penal colony and are considered further in Chapter 5.

However in the mid-May 1785, during the course of the Beauchamp Committee hearings, the government appeared to be without a site at all. In the interval between 12 and 25 May the notion of settling convicts in Das Voltas Bay emerged. The source of the proposal is not clear. The instructions to the commander of the *Swallow* in 1783 had required him to survey the south-west African coast north from Das Voltas Bay to the Portuguese settlements in Angola, and in the same year Commodore Thompson had recommended a survey of this region. It is possible Thompson himself presented this alternative to the Committee considering his subsequent involvement with the area.[49] The proposal may have been conveyed through Nepean as Frost has suggested. The Undersecretary himself indicated vaguely the background to the change of plan:

... as so much noise has been made and so many objections stated to the sending of the Convicts to the Island of Lemain, on Account of its very unhealthy situation, it may be adviseable [sic] to change the place of their Destination; the Southern Coast of Africa at or near Angra de Voltas between the Latitudes . . . is not subject to the same objections the Climate being nearly the same as Lisbon . . .[50]

It is on the basis of that loose, undated assertion that Frost has assumed the commercial and strategic motivation behind the Das Voltas Bay proposal. He has stated, without proper evidence, that Nepean was paraphrasing Thompson. That statement is a profoundly delicate fabric on which to mount the following claim:

it is the earliest indication we have of what . . . we may know to have been Pitt's acceptance of the view that they needed profoundly to increase the naval resources in the east.[51]

Since Nepean's note lists the assets of Das Voltas Bay only as fine climate and friendly natives, one is left to speculate on what strategic value it was believed to have. Reference to the questions the Beauchamp Committee put to witnesses show climate and the disposition of the inhabitants to be the principal criteria employed in selecting any convict settlements.

On 25 May John Call was brought back before the Committee. Abandoning his earlier attachment to New South Wales, he put forward a recommendation for Das Voltas Bay. Call was always aware of the direction in which the wind was blowing. Frost asserted that Call's new proposal 'can have been no other than that which Thompson gave to Sydney on 21 March'. As the details of neither proposal exist, and the reference to Thompson's plan only occurred in a diary reference, Frost's assumption is questionable. It is not adequate evidence of a concerted ministerial plan to twist the Beauchamp Committee's deliberations in favour of a site with strategic and commercial potential. The government and the Committee found themselves directed perforce to Das Voltas Bay, and in 1785 it was considered almost exclusively from a penal point of view.[52]

The subsequent meetings of the Beauchamp Committee, and any further discussions there of the Das Voltas Bay proposal, were not recorded. The final report of 21 June rehearsed some of the information in the interim report of 9 May, and went further in establishing the necessary criteria in selecting a site for a penal colony. The location needed a healthy climate and situation. It needed to be some distance from England so that return would be difficult. A coastal situation was preferred over an inland one. The site should offer means for the convicts to provide for their own subsistence after a very short time. The natives, if any, should be friendly. There should be at least the prospect of the settlement offering some return on the original investment.

In recommmending Das Voltas Bay, the Committee kept these factors clearly in mind. The region was thought to have fertile soil, a good climate, medicinal and other plants, wild cattle and hospitable local inhabitants. Its harbour was capacious, and it was relatively close to Rio de Janeiro and St Helena, and on the East India Company sea routes. The convicts could easily be shipped out in slave vessels, carrying 500 transportees each. The total cost, with six months' provisions, stock, implements and trading goods would come to no more than £23 per head. This was almost half the estimate for Botany Bay, or less than half Duncan Campbell's estimate of 1786. In all respects, therefore, Das Voltas Bay seemed to meet the government requirements.[53] Of course the information concerning Das Voltas Bay was at best conjectural, at worst imaginary. Like all promised lands, like New South Wales itself, Das Voltas Bay contained the necessities and riches appropriate to the occasion, all evidence to the contrary notwithstanding.

The Beauchamp Committee presented its report to the House on 28 July, at the end of what had been a trying Parliamentary session for Pitt. There was apparently no debate on the subject and by that time of the year the House would have been almost empty. Within a fortnight of the presentation of the report the ministry began preparations for a survey voyage to the Das Voltas Bay region. Clearly, the evidence presented to the Committee was not accepted at face value. The sense of urgency is evident from the fact that the preparations were underway before the official orders were transmitted.[54] The instructions for the voyage were to include the gathering of information on the landscape and produce of the country 'with respect to the practicality and probable advantages of making a settlement on those parts of the Coast if it should be judged expedient so to do hereafter'. The official letter to the Admiralty followed a week later.[55] The command of the surveying expedition was given to Commodore Edward Thompson. By the time the official order was issued by the Secretary of State's office, Thompson had been waiting for a year in anticipation of a patrol voyage to West Africa. His first expectation was that he would be returning to Africa to supervise the reinforcement of the various West African forts, and his vessel, the Grampus, had been kept in readiness for this until January 1785.[56] When the proposal for the Gambia was mooted, Thompson was detained further on explicit orders from the Home Office. Seemingly unaware of the Beauchamp Committee's deliberations, the Admiralty requested repeatedly that Thompson be given his instructions, since the ship was being fully manned and provisioned throughout this period. When the destination of the ship was finally decided in August, it was therefore already in a fair state of readiness.

Because of the special nature of the voyage, the government decided that a trained marine surveyor and a botanist should be included in the crew so that the Das Voltas Bay area could be properly evaluated. The surveyor was Home Popham, who was later to survey the harbour and straits of Penang, serve in the East Indies during the war, and who eventually became a knight and rear-admiral. The botanist, who was somewhat less distinguished, was the Polish refugee Anton Hove, who enjoyed the job through the patronage of Sir Joseph Banks. Banks eventually supplied draft instructions for the naturalist, which were later formalized by the Admiralty. It was also decided that Thompson should command two ships, and the sloop *Nautilus* was added to the patrol on the understanding that she should actually do the surveying work. On the issue of Thompson's instructions on 15 September the vessels were almost ready for sea. The ships sailed from Spithead on the 28th. The story of the voyage has been told in detail elsewhere.[57]

While the *Nautilus* and *Grampus* were at sea, the government sought short-term answers to the convict problem. Another small shipload was planned for Honduras, and two more hulks were commissioned. Between them these measures were to accommodate over 500 convicts.[58] On his return to London in November 1785 Richard Bradley, the agent sent out to purchase the island of Lemain, reported on the suitability of the site he had acquired on Sydney's orders. However, that option had been firmly closed. The Home Office paid Bradley off, after some delay, and seemed to place its faith in the Das Voltas option.[59]

Or did it? By the beginning of 1786 the Home Office began to manifest signs of nervousness about the Das Voltas Bay scheme, and it considered contingency plans lest the survey returned with unhelpful information. It is possible that the government contemplated the idea of sending a small contingent of convicts to New South Wales at the beginning of 1786 as a further ameliorative step in relieving pressure on the jails. At the time that the *Nautilus* was about to leave the African forts to begin her survey, Evan Nepean sought an estimate from Duncan Campbell for shipping 270 convicts to Botany Bay.[60] Those negotiations went on in haste and in secret during January. The proposal was for one ship of about 750 tons with a crew of seventy and a guard of thirty marines. The full cost of the operation was put at £13 611.12.2d or £50.8.2d for every convict sent out. The estimate included eight months' provisions for the convicts, but there was no intention to include a guardship with the contingent. Understandably, Campbell requested that the figures be kept secret.

If a firm intention to send a shipload of felons to New South Wales early in 1786 existed, obviously it did not eventuate. Perhaps Campbell's estimate suggested that economies of scale militated against sending one shipload only. Certainly the contingent possibility was not abandoned, as there seemed to be a firm resolve by the government to renew transportation in 1786 as an act of general policy, irrespective of the outcome of the Das Voltas survey. In May Pitt made a commitment to that effect to the independent MP John Rolle. One month later the Home Office undertook a review of a number of transportation alternatives, as well as schemes for employing 600 convicts in Scottish coal mines and the Woolwich ropeyard. The clearest indication of the determination to renew transportation was in a letter from Nepean to the Treasury on 10 June. Even before the ships returned from Das Voltas Bay, the Home Office had sought estimates for shipments to that region. In forwarding these to the Treasury, Nepean added the following rider:

It seemed to me to be Mr Pitt's intention at all events that if Cape Voltas was not found to correspond with our expectations for the Settlement of the Convicts that some other Spot should be fixed upon to the Southward of the Line, and as that is his determination, it might not be improper to Contract for Cape Voltas under certain conditions, that if it should be thought adviseable before the departure of the Ships from hence to fix upon some other place, that such Ships should in that case be hired at so much per Ton per Month.[61]

This revelation of the government's position makes the strategic arguments for the choice of Botany Bay extremely improbable. Was Pitt's sense of global strategy so vague that any spot 'Southward of the Line' would be adequate for the defence of India? Pitt's strategic thinking, while not profound, was not as poor as that. Nepean's letter pointed to the imperative requirement to dispose of the convicts at the most readily available site in the Atlantic, Indian or Pacific Oceans without reference to strategy or trade—financial considerations were all that constrained the choice of site. Apparently the convict problem had become so acute by the middle of 1786 that New South Wales had been established as the reserve option, in spite of the high costs involved. If the government were obliged to use that option, attention would have to be diverted from the huge financial commitment entailed by the choice of New South Wales.

On 23 July the sloop *Nautilus* put into Spithead under the command of Thomas Boulden Thompson, son of the Commodore.[62] The latter had died on the West African coast, a victim of the climate and disease which he had described so accurately to the Beauchamp Committee. His death spared him the embarrassment of explaining to the Secretary of State why the optimism about Das Voltas Bay had been misplaced. As the Portuguese had known for over 200 years, the coastal area of south-west Africa was principally sandy desert, bereft of water or vegetation. Hove, the botanist on the *Nautilus*, returned with a collection which offered scant hope to potential colonizers. While in Pequena Bay, Thompson's journal reported forlornly: 'Mr. Hove's botanical researches were attended with no success, the only plant growing here being a small Geranium.'[63]

The Commander was detained in London for debriefing for three weeks—a period prolonged by the confusion caused by Margaret Nicholson's assassination attempt upon the King. In this interval the news of the survey rapidly spread around London and on 6 August Blankett put forward his proposals for Madagascar and Tristan da Cunha as alternatives. However the ministry already had its fall-back position prepared, indicated by Howe's indifferent response to Blankett.[64] It is probable that Sydney made his report and recommendation to one of the regular Tuesday cabinet meetings (on 15 August), for by the 18th the order to the Treasury for Botany Bay had been prepared and sent.[65] Unofficial orders had already been given to the Admiralty to find suitable naval vessels to accompany the convoy.

As a response to pressures from many directions, the Pitt ministry had staggered from one remedy to another in seeking a solution to the convict problem. Options opened up and then were closed by truculent colonists, critical parliamentarians or negative surveys. In the course of this process the government found itself propelled towards what in many respects was the worst possible alternative—the scarcely-known shores of Botany Bay. Having arrived at this choice almost by default, it was then compelled to try to justify a decision which in reality had little to recommend it.

Chapter 5

THE BOTANY BAY DECISION, 1786–7

The despatch of the first fleet to Botany Bay was a reckless act on the part of a desperate ministry. The intended site for the settlement was insufficiently known; the expedition itself was poorly organized and badly equipped; the government conception of how the outpost would operate was inadequate and narrow. In the period from the order to the Treasury of 18 August until the fall of the Pitt ministry in 1801, nothing in government actions or statements suggested that the colony was founded other than for penal reasons.[1]

Sending out the first fleet without an adequate preliminary survey was irresponsible, and indications exist which suggest that the ministry and its officials were apprehensive about the consequences. The original journals of Captain Cook and Joseph Banks were ambivalent about the coast of New South Wales. Cook's observations in particular referred to the facilities available to visiting ships, rather than to the potential for colonization.[2] However the government had not drawn on these observations—indeed the order to the Treasury was confused as to which of Cook's three voyages had surveyed the coast, and referred to 'persons who accompanied him during his last voyage'.[3] Their faith in Botany Bay was based substantially on Banks's testimony in 1779, and on Matra's plan and testimony.

Although in 1786 and 1787 the government proceeded on the basis that the colony would be self-sufficient in a very short space of time, it recognized the possibility that the Botany Bay site might prove unsuitable and have to be abandoned. Governor Phillip sought a discretionary power in his instructions to move the convicts to an alternative site should it prove necessary, and this was granted.[4] It is possible that Norfolk Island was regarded as the alternative venue. The discretionary power provided to Phillip was immediately invoked when the fleet arrived in Botany Bay.

The original intention appears to have been that the first fleet would be followed by a second before any reports had been received from New South Wales.[5] Wiser councils seem to have prevailed, for this idea was subsequently qualified in case the Botany Bay plan proved to be an expensive failure. During 1788 the Home Office turned its thoughts to finding yet another alternative site, and one less likely to incur the high costs of the New South Wales experiment. In October 1788 Sydney informed the Treasury that no more convicts would be sent to Botany Bay until reports were received from there, and that in the meantime North American alternatives were being considered.[6] Two months later Nepean reported that Nova Scotia had been settled upon as the alternative to New South Wales, and while preparations were going ahead for a second fleet, the terms of the contract were being kept flexible so that the destination could be easily changed.[7]

In February of the following year the Navy commissioners signed a contract with William Richards for the transportation of some female convicts. Richards described the terms:

I have engaged to convey them either to New South Wales or to such a part of North America as may hereafter be determined upon. The occasion of the destination not being yet fixed arises from our not receiving any account of Governor Phillip's Expedition but which is daily expected. If their accounts should be favourable the Convicts in question will be sent to New South Wales. If unfavourable to North America which will hereafter be fixed upon by the King's Order in Council.[8]

The prospects for New South Wales as a permanent penal settlement were therefore very much in doubt until Phillip's reassuring despatches arrived.

The organization and equipping of the first fleet went ahead without reference to any other purpose than the removal of convicts. Sydney's order to the Treasury of 18 August referred to the position in the jails in the same terms as the orders for the Gambia in the previous year.[9] As the *Nautilus* survey had proved negative, Botany Bay was settled upon 'as a place likely to answer the above purposes'. The total number of convicts to be carried out was 750, although 778 were actually embarked. To ensure 'subordination and regularity' three companies of marines would be stationed in New South Wales, 'so long as it may be found necessary'. The military establishment therefore was not regarded as a permanent requirement for the colony, but one related to the guarding of convicts and initial protection against the indigenous inhabitants. Once the settlement was firmly established, civilian guards or wardens presumably would take on this function. The orders to the Treasury specified the need for two years' supply of provisions and assumed that livestock and seed would be collected at the Cape of Good Hope. Further quantities of seed, stock and constructional and agricultural implements were to be provided from England. A list of these was enclosed.

These orders were sketchy in outline and for more information the Treasury Lords were referred to the controversial 'Heads of a

Plan' which accompanied the letter. The official orders to both the Treasury and the Admiralty were in part drawn from this document, particularly in the references to the provisioning and supply, and the recruitment of women from the Pacific Islands.[10] The Heads of a Plan stood in the same relationship to the official orders for New South Wales as did the document on the Island of Lemain which accompanied Sydney's orders of 9 February 1785. It was a supplementary paper intended to provide background information for the Treasury and Admiralty officials responsible for the detailed planning of the enterprise. The authorship of the paper is a matter of some doubt, but as Gillen has observed, Sydney's signature gave the authority of his approval to its proposals. Various phrases in the document suggest that the principal author was outside the government, and it reads as a recommendation to government rather than an internal memorandum. The first paragraph referred to the plan being

peculiarly adapted to answer the views of government with respect to providing a remedy from the evils likely to result from the late alarming and numerous increase of felons in this country and more particularly in the metropolis.

Later the phrase 'government should . . .' occurred, and in the section on cost, the author seemed concerned to overcome potential government objections to the proposal:

Upon the whole it may be observed with great force and truth that the difference of expence . . . that this mode of disposing of them and the usual ineffectual one is too trivial to be a consideration with government, at least in comparison with the great object to be obtained by it . . . .

It is plain that this document was designed to reassure and convince the government, and was not an internally-constructed blueprint for the penal colony. It was not unusual in this period for the Secretary of State to sanctify documents originating outside the ministry.

The manner in which the first fleet was mounted and equipped does not provide support for those historians who see compelling strategic or commercial motives for the foundation of New South Wales. In military terms the new colony was to be badly protected and undermanned. The two naval vessels sent out with the first fleet had no strategic capabilities. The *Sirius* was a worn-out converted storeship, which had some years earlier been burnt to the waterline. Her armaments were reduced for the Botany Bay expedition so that she could carry more stores. In total she mounted four 6 pound carriage guns, six 18 pound carronades, and eight swivel guns. This was similar to the armament carried by ships on voyages of discovery, and was of a type suitable for dispersing convicts or Aborigines, or firing on small boats or buildings. The weapons of the *Sirius* would have been useless against a properly armed naval sloop, much less a ship of the line.

The tender *Supply* was a lightly-armed sailing brig which had been pulled out of service at the last moment from her role as a transport vessel for the rope yards. She mounted four short 4 pound guns on her main deck, four 12 pound carronades and twelve musquetoons. The strategic importance of these vessels to the colony can be measured by Nepean's suggestion that the larger of the two could be withdrawn from Botany Bay as a cost-cutting measure once the settlement was established. This remained the government's intention throughout 1787, and was embodied in Phillip's Instructions.[11]

The marine guard for the settlement was small and inadequately armed. The choice of the marines was suspect and Ross, their Commander, attributed it to Nepean's goodwill in trying to elevate them from obscurity.[12] Events were to prove that the selection was ill-advised. The initial contingent was composed of 160 privates, twenty-four non-commissioned officers, eight drummers and nineteen officers. Their ordnance consisted of eight guns, the largest being 12 pounders, and 200 muskets.[13] The function of the marines was made quite clear in the orders to the Admiralty of 31 August 1786. Those were 'not only to enforce due subordination and obedience, but for the defence of the settlement against incursions from the natives'.[14] This force was quite inadequate for the defence of a strategic colony against the most half-hearted attack.

The garrison's ability even to perform its primary function of guarding convicts and warding off Aborigines was doubted. The Judge-Advocate, David Collins, informed his brother that the force was too small, describing it as '. . . a Force so inadequate that none of the various Offices for that Purpose in Town, will insure either Lives or Property on this Occasion'.[15] He foresaw the possibility of either the convicts or the Aborigines overwhelming the marines. Governor Phillip shared Collins' opinion of the inadequacy of the force.[16]

In order to achieve any credibility as a strategic base, the settlement in New South Wales would have required between 1500 and 2000 men entrenched in solid fortifications so as to be able to withstand attack from the sea. In bases such as the Île de France and the Cape of Good Hope, the French and Dutch also had armed militias to support the regular troops, whereas the convicts in New South Wales would themselves require guards. In querying his draft instructions in April 1787, Governor Phillip urged that the strength of the garrison always be kept in proportion to the number of convicts: he was under no illusions as to the primary purpose of the marine detachment.[17] After the first fleet had sailed, he was to find that even the small force he had at his disposal was badly equipped. From Santa Cruz he reported a shortage of musket balls and cartridge paper, and a complete dearth of armourer's tools.[18] Apart from the dubious training of Lieutenant William Dawes, there were no marines in the force with any knowledge or experience of artillery and engineering.

In every respect, the force which set out from the Motherbank in May 1787 was ill-suited for the establishment of a strategic base in the southern oceans. That, indeed, had never been the government's intention, and in the next fifteen years no attempt was made to reinforce the garrison beyond the number required to guard the convicts.

The equipping and preparation of the first fleet did not suggest any commercial motives behind the foundation of Botany Bay. Some of the transport vessels were to sail to China to pick up a return cargo of tea, but the purpose of this was to reduce the cost of the undertaking, not to open up any new trade routes. The East India Company showed no inclination to send the main body of the China fleets by any other than the regular routes. The onset of the war did not change its conservative stance, in spite of the availability of the Port Jackson facility. Because of the Company monopoly, no other British merchants would have been able to use New South Wales, although exemptions from some aspects of the monopoly were subsequently given to whalers.

The strongest commercial arguments for the foundation of the colony have been mustered behind naval stores and the possibility of supplying flax and spars to Indian shipping. Evidence for this viewpoint is so meagre and circumstantial as to be valueless. Certainly a degree of concern existed in the 1780s about the vital naval stores which Britain herself was not able to produce: hemp and flax for sail-cloth, cables and running rigging, and straight-limbed but flexible conifers for masts and spars. Throughout the eighteenth century, British diplomacy in the Baltic and Scandinavia had as its principal goal continued and easy access to such staples.[19] At the same time efforts were made to find alternatives to the traditional sources of supply. In wartime and in periods of international uncertainty, these efforts became more intensive and there can be no doubt that the 1780s saw an increase in such activity.

In the search for alternative sources of supply more attention was paid to flax and hemp than to masts and spars, since the sources of supply for the latter were greater in number. Two different approaches to the problem of alternative sources for hemp and flax were taken. The first was to promote the growth of proper varieties within England, possibly by importing seeds and plants from the main nations which produced them. The second was to find new and dependable overseas supplies of the requisite quality. Both these options were pursued within certain direct constraints. Flax and hemp were bulky commodities and the costs of transporting them any distance were high. Except in cases of dire necessity, merchants would therefore always resort to the closest source of supply—Russia.[20] On the other side, the flax actually produced in Great Britain was more suitable for linen and sacking than for naval supplies and attempts to introduce new varieties were restricted by soils and climate. Hemp was a particularly difficult crop to acclimatize. In spite of this difficulty, consistent efforts were made to encourage the growing of flax and hemp in England. Acts of Parliament of 1767 and 1781 had provided for annual bounties of up to £50 000 to stimulate production, but in the 1780s that ceiling was never reached.[21] In 1783 for example, 1 682 582 pounds was produced and £1835 was paid out in bounties. Two years later production had increased to 1 918 000 pounds yielding £2164.19.8d in bounties.[22] Most of this production was from Lincolnshire, Yorkshire, Dorset and Somerset, with smaller quantities from East Anglia, Sussex, Staffordshire and Shropshire.

Between 1783 and 1787 experiments with the Chinese variety of hemp were conducted in England. One of Joseph Banks's protegées in China, the surgeon John Duncan, shipped home a package of hemp seed with samples of the worked-up product.[23] Under the influence of Banks the Company itself became involved, and it arranged for its supercargoes in Canton to send home larger consignments of seeds so that more general experiments could be got underway.[24] These seeds were delivered to Banks for distribution. In 1786 tests were made on samples of Chinese hemp supplied by the Society of Arts. The master ropemaker at Woolwich beat and dressed comparable quantities of China and Riga hemp, and subjected them to strength tests. The Chinese variety was found to yield significantly less rope. It was harder and would therefore not absorb sufficient tar to preserve it properly. It lifted 34.5 per cent less than the Riga variety.[25] Allowing for the greater quantity of the raw product needed to produce the same amount of rope, home-grown China hemp would cost 33 per cent more than the Riga variety. Nevertheless, at the meeting which heard the ropemaker's evidence, a decision was taken to request Sydney to write to the governors of Canada, Nova Scotia and New Brunswick with orders to encourage the growth of hemp in those provinces.[26] No reference was made to New South Wales, although at this time the equipping of the first fleet was in progress.

After 1786 the Board of Trade concentrated its efforts on the option of finding sources of supply outside England, with attention being focused upon Ireland, the Canadian provinces and India. The Lord Lieutenant was asked to promote the growth of hemp for naval stores in Ireland, and it was hinted that the tariff system would be altered to encourage exports to England.[27] The prospects in Canada were extensively investigated: a number of Canadian residents gave evidence to the Board; the Governors were repeatedly urged to encourage production; and seed of Russian hemp was procured through Memel, together with instructions for the dressing of the product.[28] Throughout these investigations the Board of Trade kept in close contact with the Navy Board. After 1790, increasing attention was focused on the possibility of raising hemp in Bengal. One obstacle was that the local population showed more interest in its narcotic properties than in its suitability for ropes and cables.[29]

The pressure to reduce dependence on Russian supplies of hemp was not related solely to strategic vulnerability. Price was another important consideration. Since the beginning of the Seven Years' War the price of Russian hemp had steadily risen, reaching peaks in the years of highest demand: generally, of course, the war years. Because of the build-up of stocks during the American War, the Navy Board had purchased no hemp in 1783, 1784 and 1785. Part of the concern with hemp in 1785 and 1786 had been at the prospect of paying for new supplies at higher prices.[30] In any consideration of cost, transport charges played a significant role. In spite of its strategic significance, in 1790 the Navy Board was unenthusiastic about hemp supplies from Canada because the transport costs would lift the price significantly above that for Riga hemp—the premium Russian variety. Transport charges proved an impediment to the importation of hemp from Bengal, since bulk rather than weight or value was the chief determinant of freight costs.[31] The labour costs involved in cultivating, harvesting, and processing hemp and flax were also high. This presented problems for the raising of hemp in England and also in North America. Attempts were made in 1789 to introduce less labour intensive processing methods, but this did not lead to a substantial price reduction.[32] The dressing and manufacturing work required specialist skills and equipment. Wherever serious attemps were made to encourage production, considerable thought was given to training and equipping the workers involved.

As Bolton has pointed out, it is remarkable that in the context of the lively Board of Trade and Navy Board discussions on flax after 1783, so little attention was paid to New South Wales. During the extensive Board of Trade hearings over the period to 1801 there was only one reference to New South Wales, and this was in response to a private commercial initiative. The merchant and ropemaker, Brook Watson, suggested to the Board that New Zealand flax seed should be procured through Botany Bay so that experiments could be made on raising it in England. This suggestion was passed on to the Secretary of State in October 1789 so that orders could be sent to Phillip. A consignment of seeds was eventually sent to England in March 1791, and although these were planted the experiment was not very successful. In the numerous Board of Trade papers dealing with flax and hemp, there is no mention of the possibility of importing the raw or manufactured product from Norfolk Island or New Zealand. There are no recommendations that its cultivation or manufacture be encouraged in Australasia.[33]

References to flax which have excited some historians of the foundation of New South Wales occur in two sets of sources: first, in the promotional material, the linked Heads of a Plan and in Phillip's instructions, and second, in the despatches sent home from the colony, principally by Governor Phillip and Lieutenant Governor King.[34] The promotional material of Matra, Young and Call fell into a recognizable genre of literature of a Utopian character which envisaged the deficiencies of the old world being remedied by the profusion and fertility of the new. In Matra's original plan New South Wales was the panacea for a host of problems, and would provide manifold opportunities for development. It would be a home for American Loyalists, a trading entrepôt linking Europe to China, Japan, Korea, South-east Asia and America. It would provide access to spices and timber. It would absorb surplus British population and provide a strategic base. It would provide access to the New Zealand flax plant, which Matra described in the most glowing terms. Although the Young and Call plans were a little more compact, they were cast in the same mould. Young saw New Zealand flax as a complete substitute for Russian hemp and flax. In short, one can place no more importance on these references to flax than one can on Young's belief that New South Wales would supply indigo, coffee, tobacco, sugar, tea, silk, madder and cotton. It is important to note that Governor Phillip was concerned that experiments in cotton growing should be made in the colony, and samples of seed were actually collected at Rio de Janeiro on the outward passage.[35] No historians have yet suggested that New South Wales was founded to supply raw cotton for England's industrial revolution.

The Heads of a Plan and Phillip's instructions are of more significance since they were official documents relating to the mounting of the Botany Bay expedition. However, the comments on flax in the Heads of a Plan were a paraphrase of Matra's earlier comments, and were followed by more condensed references to New Zealand timber and the potential supply of tropical products. These products, it was assumed, 'in a few years may render our recourse to our European neighbours for those productions unnecessary'. This statement is reminiscent of Sir Joseph Banks's schemes for the interchange of tropical plants.[36] The reference to flax was slightly confusing: although it was described as a New Zealand product, the document seemed to assume that this flax would be cultivated in New South Wales. This confirms Atkinson's view that there was much government confusion over the respective whereabouts of, and relationship between, New Zealand, Norfolk Island and New South Wales.[37]

In the context of the total failure of the government to provide any material support for the cultivation of flax in Australasia, one must regard the references to flax in the Heads of a Plan as a smokescreen, or makeweights designed to strengthen the arguments for, and weaken the opposition to, the Botany Bay scheme. The apparent concern with flax was all part of the politically necessary process of confusing the real cost of transporting convicts. Without any other tangible benefits arising from the penal colony the financial outlay on the enterprise looked extravagant and un-justified. Driven by desperation to an expedient it had sought to avoid, the Pitt ministry then found itself obliged to defend and justify the decision.

The reference to flax in Governor Phillip's final instructions was even more confused and vague than that in the Heads of a Plan, although its origins were more clear. The flax plant was to be found 'in the islands not far distant from the intended settlement'.[38] Did this refer to Norfolk Island or to New Zealand, or to both or indeed to either? Norfolk Island was later referred to in the singular, al-though the gaps left in the manuscript for the latitude and longitude suggested a great deal of confusion over its real location. Phillip was asked to attend to the cultivation of the flax, presumably this time in New South Wales, and to send samples home. The next portion of the instructions dealt with the occupation of Norfolk Island, but made no reference to the growing of flax there. The entire section on flax paid little more than lip service to a proposition which had in fact been put forward for ulterior reasons. Nothing was done subsequently to enable Phillip to give it practical force.

It is equally apparent that the references to flax in the instructions were the result of Phillip's own promptings. On 1 March 1787 he listed for Nepean items which he wished to be dealt with in his instructions. Among these was a request for a ship to go to 'Char-lotte Sound in the Island of New Zeland [sic]' for the flax plant.[39] Phillip's geographical knowledge seemed no more extensive than that of the Home Secretary and his officials. Perhaps he was leaving the chore of reading Cook's journals for the tedious voyage out to his new colony.

The beating and dressing of flax and hemp, and the manufacture of ropes and sailcloth were technically difficult and labour-intensive processes in the eighteenth century. Raw hemp also tended to rot in shipment, even from regions as close as the Baltic, and for it to survive a longer journey it would need to be worked up with the requisite amount of pitch or tar to preserve it. Had the Pitt ministry been truly interested in developing flax production in New South Wales, some provision for its cultivation and processing would have been apparent in the equipment of the first fleet and subsequent fleets, and in the hiring or transporting of men with the requisite technical skills. There is no evidence of this. The first fleet was not properly equipped with the stores and implements needed for sus-taining basic subsistence, much less the tools for working up naval stores.[40]

Frost has argued that the selection of the *Sirius* and the *Supply* for New South Wales service was partly geared to strategic necessity and the carriage of naval stores.[41] This argument has no substance. Both were chosen for their low cost, carrying capacity and availability. The *Supply* was not in fact the preferred choice for the job, but was selected as the only vessel which was readily available at the time.[42] Frost has also argued that the appearance of William Dawes on the first fleet was an indication of the government's firm intentions on naval stores. However, Dawes was first brought to the attention of Nepean through Banks, as a man eager for adventure, and with a knowledge of languages, botany, astronomy, mineralogy and draughting. He had no experience in the preparation of naval stores, and was never put to the task. The recommendation of him by Captain Twiss, to which Frost refers, scarcely suggested that he had such an aptitude. Twiss suggested that Dawes would assist in 'whatever You desire him to do respecting the Flax, from New Zeland [sic], or any other important Article of Commerce, which that Country may produce'. Twiss was tailoring his recommendation to fit the supposed job, and endorsing Banks's views on Dawes's enthusiasm and general talents. Dawes remained at Port Jackson to run the observatory and perform engineering tasks.[43]

There were no other persons with experience of hemp dressing, ropemaking or sailcloth making sent to New South Wales on the first fleet, and I have not been fortunate enough to find the hemp dressers and ropemakers whom Frost discovered in the occupational listings in Cobley's *Crimes of the First Fleet Convicts*. There were only five weavers on the ships; two of these were silk weavers; two more from Wiltshire and Lancashire were probably weavers of cotton and wool; the fifth from London is not further distinguishable. Roger Morley, supposedly a master weaver, was employed as a store keeper on Norfolk Island. Governor Phillip, on his arrival in New South Wales, asked for flax dressers to be sent out in terms which suggested that there were none on the first fleet.[44]

In preparing the first fleet the Pitt ministry therefore made no attempt to foster the production of naval stores for either England or India. Of course it did hope that the new colony would eventually produce enough linen to clothe its own population, although it provided scant assistance to achieve that goal. The ministry was much too pragmatic to believe that the colony could supply strategic resources. Whether shipped to England or India the raw hemp or flax would have to be fully processed into rope, cable and sailcloth so as to prevent it from deteriorating on the voyage. Even so, the high freight costs on items of such bulk would have made it uneconomic in either market. As East Indiamen generally sailed in ballast on their outward voyages, most of the stores for the Navy in India were carried out from England at reasonably competitive rates. Most of the local commercial shipping in Indian waters used ropes and running rigging made from coir, which some experts believed to be superior to hemp.[45]

It is also difficult to understand why the British government would want to encourage the dubious possibility of producing naval stores from New Zealand flax, when hemp grew naturally in India. Varieties of flax also grew there. During the French revolutionary wars the Board of Trade, the East India Company and Sir Joseph Banks began a programme to produce naval stores in India, based on the availability of these raw materials and cheap Indian labour. In the course of this exercise different types of hemp were experimented with in the Calcutta Botanic Garden; seeds of European strains were sent out to India; shipments of Indian cordage were sent to England for testing, and six Lincolnshire men trained in the industry were sent out to Bengal to supervise operations. Although these experiments can only be described as qualified failures, the determined approach of the parties involved contrasts sharply with the experience of New South Wales.[46]

The equipping of the first fleet gave no indication of a commercial or strategic purpose behind the foundation of Botany Bay. On the contrary, the preparations for the voyage reinforce the view that the urgency of the convict problem was the predominant consideration. This is evident in the selection of convicts for transportation, the proposed structure of government in New South Wales and the nature of the economy envisaged for the colony.

In selecting convicts for the first fleet, and for that matter the second and third, no thought was given to the potential development of New South Wales, or even to the immense problems of surviving in the new land. The known occupations of the convicts make it plain that no selection process on this basis occurred. There were few convicts with any skilled background in farming; one described himself as a farm labourer, another as a hay-maker and two as gardeners. There were few skilled tradesmen from the building industry: one bricklayer, one brickmaker and a brickmaker's labourer; one stonemason, three carpenters and one carpenter's labourer, and two plasterers. Among the few other skilled tradesmen there was only one fisherman, one shipwright, one caulker, one baker, three miller's labourers, one blacksmith and one mine labourer. However, these figures are a little deceptive. The stonemason was arrested and tried at the age of fifteen and had been in prison since 1783. One of the gardeners was seventeen when imprisoned. The fisherman was imprisoned at nineteen and had spent four years incarcerated. The skill level of all these men was likely to be low. There are suggestions that many others were labourers or journeymen in trades, rather than masters or artisans. There were many transportees from the clothing and textile industry, and provided the proper materials were available, the citizens of New South Wales could expect to be well-dressed. Whether the seven mantua makers would find adequate employment is a moot point.[47]

The majority of the convicts were labourers, domestic servants or were listed as having no occupation. There were also many others from itinerant occupations—hawkers, pedlars and barrow-women. Although some of the labourers were probably farm workers, or may have been linked to the construction industry, the levels of skill would not be high. After all, under the eighteenth-century criminal justice system, respectability was the only acceptable plea in mitigation and therefore it was in the interests of the defendants to state their occupations in as flattering terms as possible.[48]

On his arrival in Port Jackson Governor Phillip certainly confirmed the low level of skill among the convicts.[49] He could find only two farmers and faced a drastic shortage of carpenters, masons and bricklayers. He urged that only skilled convicts be sent out on the next fleet, and that free settlers with farming experience be recruited to promote agriculture. Unbeknown to the Governor, the government was pursuing a diametrically opposed policy. Convicts with any skills, particularly in construction and engineering, were being sifted out from the transportees for work on the Duke of Richmond's ordnance projects at the naval ports.[50]

In fact in late 1786 the convicts were emptied out of the hulks and metropolitan jails, and into the transports without any consideration of their capacities as colonizers. The principal object was to relieve pressure on the jails in the most effective way. As soon as the hulks were emptied they were filled up again with prisoners from the most crowded and unhealthy jails to forestall typhus.[51] In the course of December 1786 and January 1787 this process of transfer was carried forward as quickly as circumstances would allow, and some of the transport vessels were packed beyond their intended capacity.[52] By the end of January the process was completed but supply and provisioning problems, outbreaks of disease among the transportees and marines, and delays in drawing up the final instructions and commissions put back the date of departure.

The government's general plan for the colony testified to its essentially penal character. Providing for the government of convicts posed considerable problems, and suitable precedents were not easy to find. The model eventually chosen was that of the Newfoundland Station, but even this had to be modified. The governor's powers for granting land, for example, were drawn from instructions for Nova Scotia.[53] Neither the original orders setting up the expedition, nor the Heads of a Plan specified details of the system of government.

The ministry was confused and divided on the matter—even as late as November 1786. The First Lord of the Admiralty, Lord Howe, clearly believed the new settlement could be run on purely military lines, with the soldiers amenable to martial law, and the convicts subject to the summary justice of the governor. This would include the power of the death sentence.[54] He saw no need for criminal or civil courts with a presiding judge advocate. The Cabinet discussed these issues on either the 10th or 14th of November. In early December Phillip compared the establishment to that of New-foundland, and it was certainly a fairly skeletal one. There were to be only ten civil officers in the colony, including the governor and deputy governor. The others were the deputy judge-advocate, prov-ost marshall, chaplain, surveyor of land, a surgeon and three sur-geon's mates. The governor was left in an isolated position, which was to produce trouble in later years. While the governor's com-mission spelt out his regular powers in the form of taking oaths, enforcing the Navigation Acts, pardoning and reprieving, dealing with lunatics, granting land, declaring martial law and dealing with pirates, it was rather vague on the questions of raising money and dealing with the civilian inhabitants.

No consideration was given to the future economy of the settle-ment. Certainly, there was no indication that any staple commodity was likely to be produced. The tenor of the official documents relating to the despatch of the first fleet pointed to the creation of a subsistence economy in New South Wales, based on communal farming. The Heads of a Plan referred to 'the live stock and grain which may be raised by common industry on the part of the new settlers'. The labour of the convicts was to be pooled and superin-tended, although the ministry refused to supply the superintendents in spite of Phillip's persistent pressure.[55] His final instructions re-quired him to have the servitude of the convicts assigned to him by the masters of the transport vessels, and to put the convicts to work cultivating the land under the supervision of overseers. These were to be drawn from among the convicts themselves. Livestock was to be regarded as a community asset, and all products deriving from the labour of the convicts was to be regarded as public stock over which Phillip had absolute control. A number of convicts were to be set to work cultivating the flax plant. During his governorship Phillip generally used the convict labour as directed.[56]

Phillip was diligent in his efforts to provision and equip the first fleet, but in spite of his vigilance there was much that was slipshod. As the Comptroller of the Navy recognized, the contracts with the shippers left the convicts extremely vulnerable, as the profit was to be made only on the freight and victualling, and not on the number of convicts landed alive and well in New South Wales.[57] This prac-tice represented an unwelcome departure from customary arrange-ments in transportation to America, when the labour of the convicts had been a valuable commodity to the contractor. The true and horrifying deficiencies of the new system were to be revealed by the second fleet.

The general desire to reduce the cost of the undertaking, to-gether with the contract terms, resulted in the first fleet being inadequately supplied with stores and provisions. In the course of the preparations, Phillip had cause to complain about the inad-equacy of the medical supplies, agricultural implements, ordnance stores, victualling (particularly the meat, bread and flour), the convicts' clothing, the antiscorbutics and the wine. Some of the ships were improperly fitted out and others were carrying more convicts than was specified. Painstaking though he was in trying to remedy these defects, Phillip did not have complete success and he met frequently with an obstructionist attitude from officialdom. As a result many deficiencies remained when the fleet sailed on 12 May 1787 and the Governor was obliged to live with the consequences.[58]

The conclusion here therefore is that the period between 18 August 1786 and 12 May 1787, when the first fleet was being prepared, provides abundant evidence that the disposal of the convict problem was the government's predominant concern. Very little evidence is revealed of a commercial or strategic motive behind the foundation of Botany Bay. This is apparent from the stated intentions of ministers and officials, but more particularly in the steps taken to give force to those intentions. It is in this critical latter aspect that the arguments of the Whig historians have fallen down. When we turn to examine the true nature of Britain's strategic position in the east and on the sea routes to India, the scant importance of Botany Bay to these considerations is again sharply highlighted.

Chapter 6

STRATEGY, COMMERCE AND THE ROUTE TO INDIA

The most recent attempt to fit the founding of Botany Bay into a pattern of wider imperial purpose focuses upon the strategy appropriate to the defence of Britain's Indian empire. The account argues that fearing an increase of French naval power in the Atlantic, the Indian Ocean and eastern seas, or a combination of French and Dutch power, British planners took decisive steps to implement countervailing measures. The nature of the threat, and the British reaction to it, has been described by Frost in the following terms:

> As peace returned, France moved to strengthen her position and to weaken Britain's, especially vis-a-vis India.
>
> Pitt and his advisers saw well that France's profound purpose was (as a French agent asserted) 'to prepare the way for decisive blows in concert with the United Provinces about the coast of India'; and progressively more alarmed by the threat, they sought ways of counteracting it.[1]

This argument sees the Peace of 1783 as opening a window of vulnerability for Britain in the Atlantic and eastern seas. Despite her own best efforts in the diplomatic field, she had been obliged to hand back the conquered Dutch base of Trincomalee in Ceylon, and retained in its stead Negapatanam; a much less satisfactory alternative. The Dutch remained secure in their hold over the Cape of Good Hope. The French meanwhile were investigating possible bases from the Red Sea and Persian Gulf on one side of India, to the Philippines on the other. Between 1784 and 1789 ten French naval expeditions were at work on surveys of the eastern seas.[2] The possibility of future collusion with the Dutch was being actively investigated, and reached a peak with the Treaty of Defensive Alliance ratified at Versailles on 21 December 1785. In Frost's view, this alliance marked the nadir of Britain's influence in Europe in the 1780s, and represented a real and severe threat to British power in India, and the sea routes to the east. British ministers manifested genuine alarm at the growing menace of Franco-Dutch power and took firm measures to meet it. In Frost's opinion these measures included the establishment of a strategic base at Botany Bay:

> Knowing that control of India turned about the naval question of who commanded the eastern seas, they claimed territories and established strategic outliers to increase their capacity to defend their possessions. In the process they found a use for the convicts.

and:

> Pitt and his colleagues took this decision after an extensive and careful consideration; and their broad motive for it was the same as that for the earlier interest in Das Voltas Bay. Botany Bay was a place where they might use the convicts' labour to increase the nation's capacity to protect her position and commerce in the East.[3]

The argument here is that Frost has exaggerated the scale of the French naval threat in the Atlantic and the east; that he has exaggerated the reaction of British ministers to the threat; but more fundamentally, that he has completely misunderstood the measures which were appropriate and realistic in meeting such a threat. When studying this particular period, there is a considerable danger of becoming a belated victim of the propaganda of the Pitt ministry. It is possible to confuse a pathetic and partial pretext for an unwise or expensive decision with the true motive for it. Discrete proposals can too easily be linked into one central purpose because they are proximate in the archival record. Pitt and his colleagues did not record all their decisions on paper (no eighteenth-century governments did), and historians have been obliged to piece the story together from the surviving evidence. This process carries with it obvious dangers, and in the present context the contention is that the story of Britain's interest in the south Atlantic and the eastern seas in the 1780s has been confused, and the true origins of the penal colony in New South Wales have been obscured.

This chapter examines the sea route to India, and the nature of the British interest in the south Atlantic. The next chapter investigates the strategic problems presented by the Indian empire itself. It is argued that Britain sought to maintain its traditional interests largely by traditional means, and at no stage sought to include New South Wales in a strategic network for the defence of India.

Once Captain Cook had destroyed the vision of a southern continent, British interest in the south Atlantic and its coasts focused on two main needs. The first was the traditional problem of securing the sea lanes to India and the passage around the Cape of Good Hope. The second was the concern to open up commercial possibilities in the Pacific without precipitating a crisis with Spain, such as that which ensued over the Falkland Islands between 1765 and 1774. The policy of successive British ministers was largely reactive rather than concerted, as the Nootka Sound crisis revealed.

The security of the sea route to India was a complex problem without a simple solution. Traditionally, the answer had been a convoy system in wartime, and the maintenance of a small number of strategic bases situated along, or adjacent to the sea routes.[4] Each season more than thirty East India Company vessels set out on their voyages to India and China. By 1783, they had followed roughly the same route for more than a century: one dictated by the winds and the conservatism or caution of the ships' commanders. Leaving the Channel, the vessels pursued a triangular passage down the Atlantic; through the Bay of Biscay and south towards the Canary and Cape Verde Islands, where they would pick up the north-easterly winds which would carry them close to the Brazilian coast. From here they headed down the South American coast until they harnessed the prevailing westerlies which would carry them around the Cape of Good Hope. In the Indian Ocean the route was either through the Mozambique Channel towards Bombay and Ceylon, or well to the east of Madagascar for Madras or Bengal. The return passage was essentially the same, with more frequent calls at the Cape of Good Hope in peacetime, and often at St Helena as well. Homebound vessels would not normally sail so close to South America as ships on the outward passage.

In wartime the vulnerable points on this sea route were the Channel itself, the Cape of Good Hope, and the early passage through the Indian Ocean. The threat came from privateers and warships preying on East Indiamen from Channel bases, the Cape and the Île de France. One answer at all these points was the convoy system, but this was generally confined to European waters and homeward fleets from St Helena. Another answer was the seizure of the Cape and Île de France upon the commencement of hostilities, before they could be reinforced. Yet a third possibility was the establishment of a British base for refreshment and supply astride the sea route to India. There were some attempts in the 1780s to improve St Helena as a place for refreshment, but that island had a number of disadvantages, not least its location for outward bound ships.[5] The important point to be noted is that the location of a suitable base would not preclude an attack on the Cape, which would always remain a danger to shipping if in the wrong hands.

During the war for American independence all the possibilities listed above were considered. The convoy system was adopted as a matter of course, and in 1781 a squadron under Commodore Johnstone carried out a badly-managed attack on the Cape of Good Hope. This failure enabled the French under de Suffren to reinforce the Dutch garrison and hold it for the duration of the war.[6] Aware that his failure had exposed India fleets to attack, Johnstone sought an alternative base and refreshment place, settling eventually on the available but comparatively useless island of Trinidada off the Brazilian coast. Unmoved by Johnstone's description of it as 'an invaluable Jewell in His Majesty's Crown', the Admiralty and the East India Company Directors showed no enthusiasm for annexing the island.[7]

Nevertheless, even while the attack on the Cape was underway, ministers had been considering the possibility of finding suitable Atlantic bases as alternatives. In January 1782 Secretary of State Hillsborough shared his concern with the Chairman of the East India Company:

> The numerous Enemies we now have increase the difficulties and dangers of Navigation and require the utmost attention and foresight. It may therefore be requisite to point out where water and refreshment can be had between England and the Cape.[8]

Apparently unwilling to spare a naval frigate or sloop for the task, Hillsborough suggested that one of the Company's packet vessels survey some south Atlantic islands and unclaimed African coasts adjacent to the sea routes.

Although the Directors accepted this proposal, it was not until the autumn of 1783 that the plan was underway. In September the East India Company packet *Swallow* left England for the south Atlantic. The instructions to the commander focused upon the islands and coasts which were to be the areas of concern later in the 1780s, and which had figured in Hillsborough's letter of 1782. The ship's main objective was to be the Isla Grande, described by the London merchant Antoine de la Roche in 1675, sighted by the Spanish merchantman *Leon* in 1756, and first proposed as a desirable place for settlement by Alexander Dalrymple in 1772. The island was thought to lie in the middle of the south Atlantic. It was rich, fertile, and according to the various reports, was between six and forty miles long. Leaving the Isla Grande, the *Swallow* was to chart and examine Tristan da Cunha, before surveying the African coast between Cape Voltas at 28 degrees south and the first Portuguese settlements in Angola.

In many respects the *Swallow* was ideal for such work. Built in Bombay in 1777, she was a teak-hulled vessel of 345 tons, a good sailer, and fast for her size. As it transpired, she was not fast enough for the task demanded of her. The intention was that she should return to England in time to provide information to the outward-bound India and China ships in the spring, but September was not the month to beat against the prevailing south westerlies in the Channel and Bay of Biscay. The *Swallow* reached the Brazilian coast too late in the season to conduct a useful survey, and headed for St Helena before returning home.

The ending of the war and signing of the Peace Treaty reduced British fears about the security of the sea passage to India, but did not completely remove the traditional object of concern. The Cape was restored to Dutch control and British shipping began calling there again, particularly when in need of fresh vegetables and live-stock. However, the precarious situation in the Netherlands did not allow room for complacency, since the French were eager to con-clude a defensive alliance with Holland which would offer a poten-tial threat to Britain. In the autumn of 1785 French links with the Patriot Party were cemented and in December a formal alliance between the two countries was ratified. Early in the new year the French-backed Patriots gained control of the ailing Dutch East India Company.

It is apparent that the most profound implications of the French involvement in the Netherlands would be felt in Europe itself and would present a direct threat to the British Isles. This was, of course, a traditional problem, and had been the central feature of British diplomacy and strategic thinking for more than two centuries. It had been the focal point of alliances in Europe, and significantly in the 1780s Britain found she had few friends and potentially many enemies. So vital was this issue to England's immediate security that Pitt was ultimately prepared to go to war in the case of direct French intervention.[9]

There was an imperial dimension to this crisis, and it had the most serious implications for Britain's eastern empire. This has been one of the central themes of Alan Frost's *Convicts and Empire*, as noted in numerous instances. The basis of this argument is that the French would reinforce and control the Dutch bases from the Cape of Good Hope to the Spice Islands, and thereby present a serious threat to British power in India, and to the trade to China. Ulti-mately this threat could only be met by strengthening the Navy in Indian waters, and by the capture of French and Dutch bases. At the height of the crisis in the Netherlands in the summer of 1787, plans were mapped out for a pre-emptive attack on the Cape and Trincomalee, in the name of the Stadtholder.[10] The establishment of additional British bases on the route to India and China, or in eastern seas, would not have obviated this need although provided they were well placed, such bases might have improved strategic flexibility.

In the mid-1780s the possibility of establishing bases in the south Atlantic was raised in the context of the convict problem. Although there can be no doubt of the primary concern of the Beauchamp Committee and the ministry at that time, strategic considerations were put forward as supplementary factors in assessing the sites.

The Beauchamp Committee had recommended Das Voltas Bay in south-west Africa. As well as being ideal for a penal colony, the Committee pointed out that a settlement there would be an in-valuable refreshment place on the sea routes to the east, particularly for homeward bound Indiamen and for the southern whale fisher-men. It would also serve as a suitable base for naval vessels, and provide an alternative, as well as a potential threat to the Cape of

Good Hope. This supplementary purpose for the proposed settlement was in line with the Committee's view that a penal colony should be of some value to the mother country, and that convict labour should be put to some use. In its own words, the intention was to 'fix upon such Spots for the transportation of Criminals as may by the Commercial and Political advantages to be derived from them indemnify the Public for the Original charge'.[11] The criteria here established later embarrassed the ministry in the context of the New South Wales decision.

The expedition of the sloop *Nautilus* between February and May 1786 was intended to survey this favoured spot, but in fact it discovered little but desert and treacherous shores. With the failure of this mission the Pitt ministry was obliged to settle on an alternative site for a convict colony. In spite of considerable misgivings, it switched its attention to the distant land of Botany Bay. In doing so Pitt and his colleagues in no way believed that it was possible for this site to offer one and the same strategic possibilities as a south Atlantic base.

While at the height of the crisis in the Netherlands the British government considered more direct answers to the strategic threat in the east, by the middle of 1789 they had turned their thoughts once more to the secondary possibility of alternative bases in the south Atlantic or on the African coasts. Although this was essentially the restatement of a traditional need, there was also a new element which widened the scope of the search and increased the pressure on government. An aggressive British whaling industry required refreshment places near their passages into the Pacific and Indian Oceans, and was petitioning the government for assistance.

The southern whale fishery was a rapidly expanding industry in the 1780s owing to the exclusion of the enterprising Nantucketers from the British market after the American War for Independence. As an infant concern, the industry sought (and generally secured) government support in the form of financial incentives and the removal of geographical restraints on their right to fish. The prey of these whalers was generally the pelagic sperm whale, a wide-ranging mammal which retreated before the fishing onslaught, drawing the ships ever further from their home ports. As each region was fished out, or the whales became more canny, the ships were lured to new regions bordering on the Pacific and Indian Oceans. At this point they ran up against the exclusive monopolies of the South Sea and East India Companies.[12]

In January 1786 the leading firms in the fishery approached the Treasury for financial assistance in the form of bounties, and for the right to sail into the Indian and Pacific Oceans. The Treasury in turn referred the request to the Privy Council Committee for Trade and Plantations, which began hearings on the question in February. From the outset the government attitude was encouraging. The fishery was regarded as one of those vital 'nurseries of seamen' which were so important for Britain's naval strength. A system of premiums was agreed upon, and under ministerial pressure the South Sea and East India Companies agreed to relax their monopolies. An Act for the Encouragement of the Southern Whale Fishery embodied the changes. In 1788 the Act was amended to increase the premiums and extend the freedom to fish in the Indian and Pacific Oceans.[13]

As the whaling frontier moved outward the industry soon felt the need for bases for refreshment and processing. One possible difficulty here was the risk of offending Spain. A party of sealers had been left on Staten Island off Tierra del Fuego in 1787, and on their return to London in July 1788, the leader of this group had belatedly sought information from the government on Spanish rights in this area.[14] In the same year Samuel Enderby and Sons, wishing to send their vessel *Emelia* around Cape Horn, sought information from Sir Joseph Banks on possible places of refreshment and the question of Spanish rights.[15]

Attention to these concerns was focused rather more sharply in April 1789 when Spanish frigates caught two British whalers repairing their vessels at Puerto Deseado on the Patagonian coast. In this case the ships involved, the *Sappho* and the *Elizabeth and Margaret* were merely ordered away with a warning that the 'Public Seas' off the South American coast were exclusively Spanish territory.[16] Alarmed by such broad Spanish claims, the whalers petitioned the Secretary of State for Foreign Affairs and the President of the Board of Trade to take up the matter with the Spaniards. For its part the Board of Trade regarded the claims as nonsense, and it urged the Duke of Leeds to defend the British right to fish in open seas, and to use uninhabited regions for refreshment. There was an obvious need for a base where the whalers could refresh without hindrance.[17]

With this additional pressure to consider, Lord Grenville, the new Secretary of State for Home Affairs, began to re-examine the need for a base in the south Atlantic. As a first step the plans for the Swallow voyage of 1782–3 were retrieved and discussed. Eventually this formed the basis for a new expedition to the south Atlantic.[18]

From the outset it was clear that this was to be a more elaborate and more carefully-planned survey than its predecessor. Advice on such a survey had already been received from Captain Blankett in June, and in August discussions began informally between Evan Nepean and Sir Joseph Banks on the scope and scale of the voyage. By 27 August Banks had already chosen the botanist Archibald Menzies as scientific officer to the expedition.[19] Little further action seemed to be taken in September, but on 3 October Grenville officially informed the Admiralty of the nature of the expedition and ordered a proper ship to be fitted out as quickly as possible, so that it might sail during the winter.[20] He outlined the purpose of the voyage in these rather vague terms:

... certain Islands situated in the Southern Atlantic Ocean, and comprised within Cape Horn and the Cape of Good Hope, as well as some parts of the Coast of Africa, should be examined with a view to further operations.

Enclosed with this order were the draft instructions to the commander of the vessel. Isla Grande was once more the focus of attention, and traverses eastward in the region of latitude 45 degrees south were to be made in search of it. Once found, the island was to be charted and its soil, vegetation and water supply were to be examined thoroughly. Having completed this part of the mission, the commander was to sail to St Helena to hand charts to the Governor before returning to the survey. The next sweep was to be further north, and to include Tristan da Cunha, which was to be charted and examined, and the recently discovered Gough's Island. The African part of the survey was to embrace the area covered by the *Nautilus* in 1786, and the eastern coast between the Dutch territory and the first Portuguese settlement in Mozambique.

The objectives of this voyage were similar to those of the *Swallow* in 1782–3, but the scale had increased. Now that the convict problem was resolved, the strategic consideration was again uppermost in the minds of the ministry. This was reflected in the regions to be surveyed, which were all adjacent to the sea routes to the east. The settlement at Botany Bay had no influence at all on the strategic thinking of the government at this time, and filled no direct need other than the rather nebulous one of pre-empting settlement by any other country.

Perhaps the most remarkable, if incomprehensible affirmation of this was in the instructions to examine south-west Africa. As far as can be determined the *Nautilus* survey had been a thorough one, although it had not gone quite far enough north. But the commander of the new ship was ordered to cover the ground again, and was given the detailed charts of Home Popham, the surveyor on the first voyage. Once the idea had been suggested in 1785, apparently the Pitt ministry saw this coast as being ideally situated for a base and were loath to abandon the idea without further investigation. Perhaps it was also seen as a suitable staging-post for an attack on the Cape of Good Hope in time of war.

Plans for the new expedition went ahead methodically in the autumn of 1789. The Navy Board had been ordered to look for a vessel of about 300 tons which could be brought into the service. Eventually they settled on a new ship on the stocks at Randall and Brent's yard at Rotherhithe.[21] A large shallop, or deckless boat, of forty tons was also constructed and readied to be put aboard the ship in frame. On 7 December the new vessel was entered on the

Navy lists as the sloop *Discovery* and her command was given to Henry Roberts, a veteran of Cook's second and third voyages. George Vancouver, another of Cook's officers, was made her first lieutenant.[22] The *Discovery* was launched on 20 December and was towed down to Deptford where she was to be fitted out and provisioned. A distinctive feature of her design was the large 'plant hutch' or greenhouse which, on Banks's advice, had been erected on her quarter deck. Here Menzies was to preserve interesting plants and seeds which were collected on the voyage.[23]

As in many other voyages in this period, Cook's voyages were regarded as something of a model, and in this case his second voyage offered particularly useful parallels. In consequence, *Discovery* was fitted, stored and manned much as the *Adventure* had been. A good selection of surveying and astronomical instruments were supplied, together with relevant charts and journals.[24] Because of the expected duration of the voyage and the nature of the seas being traversed, special rations were supplied, including the usual ineffective selection of antiscorbutics.

The original intention was that the expedition should leave in November or early December. Delays in the building and fitting of the *Discovery* kept pushing the departure date back. It was not until the end of January that she was ready for sea and by then outside events intervened to delay the expedition still further. At about that time news reached England of the Spanish seizure of British trading vessels at Nootka Sound on the north-west coast of America. A major diplomatic crisis erupted between England and Spain, and Pitt and his colleagues began preparations for a military expedition to the north Pacific in order to restore British territory and property. This was not a suitable time for a survey vessel to be prowling around the south Atlantic where there had already been incidents with Spain, and the *Discovery* voyage was therefore suspended.

Suspended, but not abandoned. Grenville maintained his interests in the expedition even during the Nootka Sound crisis. While the emergency was on, the *Discovery* was used as a receiving ship for pressed seamen, and its crew was dispersed through the fleet. After an understanding with Spain was reached on 24 July, planning for the voyage was resumed. Spanish sensitivities, coupled with the moving frontier of the whalers, had changed the requirements of the expedition. It was obvious, for example, that the whalers' difficulties could be raised in the context of the discussions with Spain. In August Grenville sought information from Samuel Enderby on Tristan da Cunha and the ports on the Pacific coast of South America. One of Enderby's ships, the *Emelia*, had been operating in the Pacific in 1789, and had returned in March of the following year with charts and valuable information about potential bases.[25] This information was used in the negotiations with Spain, and the Convention signed on 28 October guaranteed unrestricted fishing in the south Atlantic and Pacific, provided the whalers did not go within ten leagues of occupied Spanish territories. The implication of this was that unoccupied areas could be used by the whalers for refitting and for refreshing their crews.

In November the business of refitting the *Discovery* began and the decision was made to supply a smaller vessel to accompany her: the brig *Chatham*. By the end of November the destination of both ships was still the south Atlantic. On 11 December a sudden change occurred: the Admiralty ordered the *Discovery* to be paid off and on the 14th Captain Roberts accompanied his crew to the Pay Office. A few days later Roberts himself was replaced as commander of the *Discovery* by George Vancouver, and the two ships had their destination changed to the north Pacific.[26]

There are no Cabinet minutes or private letters to explain this change of plan, and one must therefore hypothesize from the known facts. The Convention with Spain provided for a restitution on the spot. This necessitated sending at least one ship to Nootka Sound. Grenville's orders to the Admiralty in December directed that two ships for this purpose be readied for sea and the decision to re-route the *Discovery* and *Chatham* seemingly had already been made. In November or December the Pitt ministry had re-sorted its priorities and decided that the restitution of Nootka provided a favourable opportunity for a survey of the north Pacific, and search for the north-west passage.

Archibald Menzies claimed that Captain Roberts was detained to go out to the south Atlantic in another vessel in the spring of 1791, and there is evidence to support this view. On 24 September Roberts wrote to Philip Stephens of the Admiralty requesting that several of the men who had been with him on the *Discovery* should be entered on the books of some other ship 'until such time as another ship is provided for the expedition'.[27] In June of 1791 Roberts was still writing to the Admiralty as though the south Atlantic expedition was in view and he was to be appointed to command it. Archibald Menzies was disenchanted with eighteen months of delay and uncertainty, and he decided to gò to Nootka Sound.

During 1790 and 1791 a number of changes had helped to reshape the strategic and commercial priorities of Pitt and his colleagues. The French Revolution had manifestly weakened that nation militarily, and this was particularly the case in the Navy. There had already been a hint of this during the Nootka crisis when France had equivocated in answering Spanish cries for help, and Louis XVI had been obliged to refer the matter to the National Assembly.[28] By the beginning of 1791 France was further weakened, and in no position to threaten the sea route to India, or India itself. British concern therefore lessened and the south Atlantic survey seemed a less pressing need.

As has already been suggested the needs of the whalers were also changing as they moved into the Pacific and Indian Oceans. The question of access to South American shores had been satisfactorily dealt with in the Convention with Spain, although there were still a few areas of doubt. During discussions with Spain another British whaler, the *Astrea*, was ordered off the Patagonian coast, and the whalers were reluctant to send ships around Cape Horn without more information on the location of Spanish settlements.[29] In January 1791 a Bristol whaler and fur trader, Sydenam Teast, sought information from the Board of Trade on the rights and privileges of ships of the Pacific American coasts. He wished to know where they could fish; where they might refit and refresh; if they were able to land to kill seals; and whether they could trade to those coasts or to Nootka Sound.[30] In the same month the Board of Trade began an investigation into the industry, and the north-west fur trade. These inquiries made it clear that the need for whaling bases had shifted to the Pacific coast of South America and Vancouver's instructions therefore required him to search for such sites on his return to England, and to try and locate the mythical Isla Grande as well.[31]

British interest in the south Atlantic therefore declined somewhat as the pressures which had generated it relaxed. In the early years of the revolutionary war with France the evident superiority of the British fleet at home and in the East Indies, and the successful seige of the French fleet at Toulon preserved the calm. It was only with the French annexation of the Netherlands that serious concern was shown and, as will be explained, this threat was met by the rapid capture of the Cape of Good Hope and Trincomalee. This offered some protection along the sea route to India.

In the course of the 1780s and 1790s Britain had exhibited considerable concern about its military position in the south Atlantic and the security of the sea route around the Cape of Good Hope. At various points the interest in the region was linked to, or confused with, other requirements such as those of the whalers, and one instance the need to resolve the convict problem. In casting about for a suitable site for a penal colony in 1785 the Beauchamp Committee had recommended Das Voltas Bay, which, since it was also close to the sea route to India, was considered of potential as a refreshment point for naval and commercial vessels. At the time the implications of the use of the site were not recognized, and the problems which a convict population might present for a strategic base were never considered. In the event the site proved unsuitable for what was intended to be its primary function—a convict colony—and the tenuous link between convicts and naval strategy was broken.

The expedition planned under Grenville's direction in 1789 had no reference to New South Wales, or to the use of convicts to form a base. Botany Bay was irrelevant to the strategic needs the survey was to satisfy: its founding had therefore done nothing to reduce British concern about the passage to India. Frost's assertion that New South Wales was some sort of strategic substitute for the proposed site at Das Voltas Bay does not withstand scrutiny.[32] When in August 1786 the Pitt ministry found itself propelled towards a Botany Bay site for a penal colony, it realized that it was in grave danger of departing from one of the Beauchamp Committee guidelines: that the convicts should be employed 'to the most useful Purposes', and that no purely penal colony should be established. There could be no pretence that convicts at Botany Bay could assist in protecting the sea routes to India. The next chapter will show they were equally irrelevant to the defence of India in eastern seas.

Chapter 7

INDIA AND THE EASTERN SEAS

The next major strategic problem requiring consideration is the protection of the British settlements on the Indian subcontinent from attack by land or by sea, and the associated question of the control of the Indian seas themselves. Here the questions which must be asked are: how deep was British concern about the vulnerability of India; how real was the French threat to the Indian empire; and what relevance, if any, did the colony of New South Wales have to the defence of British territories on the subcontinent?

In his book *Convicts and Empire* Frost sees the defensive alliance between the French and Dutch in December 1785 as throwing Dutch bases at the Cape of Good Hope, Trincomalee and in Southeast Asia open to the French. Dutch troops would be placed under French command in time of hostilities and the French forces at Pondicherry, south of Madras, and on the islands of Île de France and Bourbon in the Indian Ocean, would be augmented. The French fleet would be strengthened by the rapid conversion of warships *armé en flûte*. While these vessels were ostensibly serving as merchantmen, it seemed a relatively easy task to convert them back to their primary purpose as ships of the line.[1] While pro-French Indian states attacked British settlements by land, combined French and Dutch forces would begin the assault by sea. Desperately overstretched and under-armed, British forces on land and sea would collapse before the onslaught.[2]

The contention here is that both the scale of this threat, and the level of British concern have been greatly exaggerated. The French presence in India had been substantially weakened during the war for America, and this process continued during the 1780s. In spite of its own best efforts, relationships with former Indian allies deteriorated into muddle and mutual suspicion. When the war against Britain was renewed in February 1793, the strategic threat posed by France was soon eliminated. During the Revolutionary and Napoleonic wars the French war effort in the eastern seas was confined to privateering attacks on British commercial shipping from the Île de France and Bourbon. These were as much a matter of necessity for the supply-starved islanders as a contribution to the war effort.[3] British concern at that time was directed mainly to forestalling the French drive into Egypt and the Near East—an indirect but menacing threat to India.[4] By the time of the resumption of the war in 1803 the French naval force in eastern seas consisted of one ship of the line and three frigates: a force capable of depredatory raids but not sustained military action. From 1808 this threat was reduced to one of lesser firepower: five frigates and two corvettes. As Parkinson has observed, in response to this threat the role of the British Navy in India 'resolved itself into mere commerce protection'.[5]

The decline in French power can be traced to the American War of Independence, but was accelerated after it. Out of the Peace Treaties of 1783 there arose an informal understanding that British, French and Dutch naval forces in the eastern seas should be reduced, and that a rough parity should be achieved. In April 1783, the newly created Home Department suggested five ships of the line and two fifth-rate vessels would provide an adequate British presence.[6] The British intention was clearly to maintain a proper balance of power at sea without provoking the French into an escalation of forces. This policy could be pursued with the comforting knowledge that British land strength in India was infinitely superior to that of the French. The eventual understanding was that five ships would provide an adequate and reasonable force for each nation, provided that none of the vessels was larger than a 64-gun ship.[7]

Conflict nevertheless arose over the quality and size of these five ships, and the question of whether the agreement was being honoured. From the British perspective, the French sometimes seemed close to breaching the understanding in providing vessels *armé en flûte* for the French East India Company of Calonne. Although the lower deck guns had been removed from these beamy 64-gun warships, it seemed that these might be easily restored in time of hostilities.[8] However, in spite of the hysteria of a few spies and diplomats, there is little to suggest that the Pitt government regarded this threat as a serious one. Only three vessels were initially to be supplied to the French East India Company, although by 1787 there were reports from the Île de France of up to six being deployed.[9] However unless these ships sailed continually in squadron, with their guns ready to be mounted, or were permanently stationed at the Île de France, they could scarcely present a sustained threat. While the Pitt ministry was vigilant, and maintained its intelligence systems in the east, it reacted cautiously to alarms raised by agents in Europe. Britain had good reason to act in a measured rather than hysterical way to any French threats in eastern seas.

France, on the other hand, had less reason for complacency, and in the decade between the wars had more to fear than the British.

Her actions in the 1780s revealed fully these insecurities. Although her naval force in eastern seas was the equal of, and in some senses was superior to the British, the total volume of British shipping was much greater. It was also increasing at a rapid rate in the 1780s, especially in the trade to China. In the eyes of the French this increase in shipping could only be interpreted as a prelude to further territorial expansion. Observing the twenty-nine ships of the English East India Company loading at Canton in 1786, the French Admiral d'Entrecasteaux refused to accept them as the expression of a purely commercial purpose. Their military potential appeared to him obvious, and required effective countermeasures. He believed the number of vessels would continue to increase and they would find a wartime role:

... que l'intention des Anglais est d'accoutumer l'Europe à des expéditions aussi et plus nombreuses que celle de cette année et que ... à l'époque d'une rupture prochaine, le même nombre de vaisseaux expédiés également d'Europe sera destiné vraisemblablement ... à des expéditions d'une autre nature. Quarante vaisseaux de la force de ceux de la Compagnie destinés à transporter les nombreuses troupes qu'ils ont à la Côte Coromandel, dans toutes les possessions hollandaises par exemple, s'en seroient bientôt rendues maîtresses.[15]

Given the increase in the size of British East Indiamen the fears of d'Entrecasteaux were legitimate; at least in a naval sense. Ships in both the India and China trades grew in size in this period reaching 1200 and even 1800 tons. These were frequently pierced for 40 or 50 guns, and were strongly built and similar in size to a 64-gun ship of the line.[11] When the war resumed in 1793 six of these larger vessels were taken into the navy and equipped as men of war. Eight other East Indiamen in the process of construction were directly assigned to the navy as warships.[12] As auxiliaries to a regular squadron of battle ships they presented a threat more than equal to that of the French.

Naturally there was an element of bluff in all this. In peacetime East Indiamen (and presumably vessels *armé en flûte*) were lightly manned in comparison to ships of the line of the same size. They were generally unable to carry guns on their lower decks while laden, and the guns they did carry were mostly short-range carronades.[13] Their prime function was cargo carrying. The stowage of merchandise and working of guns were not easy functions to combine. Nevertheless on at least two occasions in the Revolutionary and Napoleonic Wars, the size of the China ships, and their resemblance to ships of the line, sufficiently confused French forces so that they preferred to retreat rather than seek an engagement.[14] In 1804 the returning China fleet under Commodore Nathaniel Dance actually fought off and gave chase to the French squadron under Admiral Linois near the Straits of Malacca.[15]

Another major problem for the French was the inadequacy of their bases, which were either badly located or impossible to defend. Until 1786 Pondicherry and the Île de France were the principal bases: after that year the force fell back to the Île de France alone. Well-placed though this island might have been with regard to the sea route to India, it was unsuitable as a station for gathering intelligence about Indian waters or mounting a large-scale attack on British settlements in India.

This is not to suggest that the British government was unconcerned by French naval activity in eastern waters. This activity was always considered in a measured way and the response was always assessed in terms of what was least likely to offend or provoke the French and Dutch. The naval force schedules of 1783 recognized that it was 'probable the French will continue a force in those seas of as great a Number of Ships as the English do'.[16] When the French Admiral Macnamara criticized the bolstering of British naval forces by the arrival of Cornwallis's squadron in Indian waters in 1789, the British reaction was one of nervous embarrassment while they sought to allay French fears.[17] As has been pointed out elsewhere, the need for caution in areas of Dutch interest was even more strongly felt, for fear of throwing the Netherlands into the arms of France.[18]

During the 1780s therefore the British government realistically assessed French activity, and where appropriate took proper countermeasures in the immediate area of threat. This did not include the establishment of a base at Botany Bay. An example of this attitude can be seen in the response to French surveying expeditions in eastern seas. When French missions were sent to the Red Sea and Persian Gulf, British surveys quickly followed, and a communication network for despatches through Suez developed.[19] French surveys further east were matched by British investigations of potential bases on Diego Garcia, the Nicobars, the Andaman Islands, which were occupied in December 1789, the Straits of Malacca, Cochin China, the Pelew Islands and north-west New Guinea.[20]

The most sustained effort of this sort occurred at the peak of the crisis in the Netherlands in 1787. Because of the uncertainties and confusion about navigation in eastern seas, Lord Mulgrave of the Board of Control had suggested a survey by some 'young intelligent officer'. In April he approached Alexander Dalrymple for information on possible bases in the seas around India, particularly in the region of Diego Garcia. Dundas immediately followed this up, and instructions were sent to Governor General Cornwallis. The purposes of this survey were quite specific and clearly stated. The commander was to find proper stations for shelter, refitting, refreshing and protecting squadrons in eastern seas in different seasons, or at different times of the year. Observations were to be made on aspects such as ease of access, potential for fortification, and quality of harbours. The particular objects of the survey were to be Diego Garcia, Sumatra, Acheen, Pulo Pinang, the Nicobars, and the harbours of Bengal, Madras, and Bombay. This task was eventually carried out by Lieutenant Moorson in the sloop *Ariel*.[21]

The Court of Directors subsequently ordered the Bengal government to establish a base at Rhio, but were pre-empted by the Dutch.[22] The settlement of Penang by Francis Light in July 1786 was intended to establish a secure British base on the passage to China and to guarantee an influence with the independent states which straddled the sea route.

Apart from exploring the possibility of establishing bases and alliances in areas immediately adjacent to settlements and sea routes, the ultimate measures necessary to control French or Franco-Dutch threats were attacks on enemy bases. In Indian and South-east Asian waters the British were in a strong position to carry out such action. In spite of the brilliant naval exploits of de Suffren, French military power in India had been weakened substantially during the American War of Independence. The military decline continued in the two decades after 1783. Pondicherry, the seat of government in India itself, was practically indefensible. In 1785 this was recognized in the Royal Edict which transferred the seat of government to the Île de France. As Sen has described it, this can be taken as 'indicating that France had definitely abandoned her ambitions in India'.[23] The garrison at Pondicherry was reduced to a Sepoy force of 1200 by the Edict—barely adequate for police duties. Four years later orders were given to further reduce this force to 500 men. The city had become a defenceless commercial outpost, with no expectation that it could be defended in wartime.

With this change came the recognition that military alliances with Indian powers did not repay the effort invested. The Peace of 1783 had compromised and discredited France in the eyes of her former Indian allies. This distrust persisted throughout the 1780s. French officers in India were all too sanguine about the prospect of adequate alliances with the Marathas, Mysore or Hyderabad.[24] Although authorities in Paris placed faith in Tipu Sultan of Mysore, officers on the spot correctly saw his violent Anglophobia as manifesting antipathy to all Europeans, and therefore considered him unreliable as an ally. The difficulty of forming Indian alliances confirmed the logic of a military withdrawal from India, and this became official policy in September 1788—a frank admission of the overwhelming military superiority of the British in India.[25]

While the essential French weakness in India was apparent to both the British government and the Directors of the East India Company, it did not leave room for complacency about Britain's own military strength. While her land forces were clearly superior to those of the French or Dutch, her naval strength was suspect. As has been pointed out, parity with the French was the most that could be claimed in terms of vessels before 1788, although Britain had more suitable naval bases, and better access to naval stores. During the period of the crisis in the Netherlands there was considerable discussion of the naval deployment in eastern seas, and the end result of these was the decision in 1788 to augment the forces in Indian waters. In October orders were given that the East India fleet should be boosted by one 64-gun ship, two frigates and a sloop. This small fleet, under the command of Admiral Cornwallis, was at Spithead ready to sail in January of the following year.[26]

However, to focus on British naval weakness in Indian waters in this period is to underestimate the diplomatic difficulties in maintaining a sizeable fleet. The Peace of 1783 had recognized the need for some sort of balance of power in Indian waters, and both France and Britain had nominally kept within the terms of this agreement before 1788. The despatch of Cornwallis's squadron was technically the first breach of the agreement, and it produced a sharp reaction from the French. Their understanding was that only vessels of frigate size and below were to be stationed in eastern waters. Their own force consisted of four frigates and two cutters at the time.[27]

The real problem for Britain was the need to avoid alarming the Dutch. The great fear was that of pushing the Dutch into an alliance with France, and the discussions within the Pitt ministry between 1784 and 1788 were preoccupied with ways of avoiding this. Dundas in particular was concerned to take all steps to avoid anything which could be seen as threatening to the Dutch empire in eastern seas.[28] While a strong land force in India itself could be seen as at most an indirect threat, a large British naval force would be seen as a direct challenge to the Dutch presence in Ceylon and the Spice Islands. A strong force would strengthen the hands of the Patriot Party in the Netherlands, and make the prospect of a firm alliance with France more likely.

Naval strategy in eastern seas therefore involved a delicate balancing act, in which the maintenance of a modest, efficient force of ships, adequate intelligence of the movements of other powers, and the maintenance of adequate bases all played a part. In the 1780s this policy was augmented by a survey of potential bases in the seas adjacent to the Indian subcontinent. Of course, in the last resort, the defence of British India would necessitate attacks on Dutch bases at Trincomalee, the Cape of Good Hope, and eventually the Dutch East Indies, as well as the capture of Pondicherry, Chandernagore and the French Indian Ocean Islands. This was the pattern of events in the wars of 1793 to 1815.

The war years throw the true military capacity of the respective powers into sharp relief, and reveal the constraints on their actions. Chance, general incompetence (or skill), winds and geography were all important to success at sea. Because of their difficulties with bases, the French were really reduced to privateering attacks on

British shipping. The Île de France proved of limited use as a base, and was frequently blockaded by the British. The north-east monsoon restricted the times of year during which ships could sail from the island. The French had no military force to supplement naval action in the east, and any attacks on land were little more than hit and run skirmishes.

The general aim of the French was to capture parts of the India and China fleets, and in this way to stretch British naval resources to the utmost. This tactic was only partially successful, and missed many opportunities. The crews of French warships were often badly nourished and poorly trained. The ships were under great strain, and were often difficult to repair. Lines of communication to France were stretched and irregular; the French commander in the east and the Governor of the Île de France could be excused for thinking that they had been forgotten. The greatest pressure which France brought to bear was during Napoleon's Egyptian campaign, when the prospect of an attack on India from that direction caused great alarm in the British camp.

Secure in their military strength in India, and with the Cape and Trincomalee in their hands by 1795, the British were able to regard the French navy as little more than a nuisance.

Throughout the period after August 1786, the important point about the role of New South Wales in this eastern strategy is its striking irrelevance. Botany Bay was thousands of miles and many months sailing away from the vital areas of interest around India and on the sea routes to China. No ships of the line were deployed at Port Jackson, or within 3000 miles of it. There was no earthly reason why any should have been. New South Wales had nothing strategically to offer, and any naval vessels resorting there would have been removed from vital and legitimate areas of concern.

The war years produced no change in this situation. Rather than finding itself incorporated into an eastern strategy, New South Wales was increasingly isolated.

Chapter 8

NEW SOUTH WALES ESTABLISHED

The bedraggled fleet which put into Botany Bay on 18 January 1788 had been launched into isolation. It was to be almost two and a half years before supplies were received from England and in the intervening period the infant colony came close to starvation. Governor Phillip must have been aware of the daunting task which faced him as he searched for a suitable site for the settlement. Problems had already been revealed in the victuals and the stores provided for the settlement. On the voyage, and in the early days of the colony, there were strong hints that the Marine Corps was to be a source of continual problems.[1]

However the true magnitude of the task Phillip faced would not have been evident to him until several months had elapsed. One difficulty arose from the expectations that had been aroused over Botany Bay. Captain Cook and his crew had provided a superficial account of the New South Wales coast line, but had not penetrated inland, or attempted to assess resources in a systematic way. Nevertheless, on these fragile foundations the promoters of settlement in New South Wales had built an impressive Arcadian vision. The region was fertile, well-watered and embraced the best possible range of climates. All manner of useful products were either indigenous or could be established there, 'uniting in one territory almost all the productions of the known world'.[2] New South Wales was ideally situated for an entrepôt, strategic base and way station. It would provide a haven for the empire's poor or dispossessed. The local inhabitants were timid and not numerous. In the view of Matra, of all new countries which held out 'the most enticing allurements' to Europeans, 'None are more inviting than New South Wales'.[3] Unfortunately, although the continent enticed, it surrendered its many treasures slowly and grudgingly.

When the first crops failed, and the coastal soils were found to be poor, and when fresh water was short and the continent was found to yield no obvious vegetable or animal products, the settlers developed a bitterness towards those who had been so fulsome in their praise of the new land.[4] Although the Governor struggled to maintain his optimism, at least in official despatches, the majority in the colony were forlorn about their prospects, and could see no possible future for the colony. Captain Campbell's view, sent to an aristocratic contact, was typical:

Surely My Lord administration will never persist in so romantick a scheme as the forcing a settlement in such a country as this at present appears to be—Not one thing can be found that ever promises to be an object of Commerce, or worthy the attention of a Commercial Nation. Did the Harbour indeed lay in passage to any of our other settlements it would then certainly be most desirable—but even then, everything necessary for equipping or repairing ships must be procured from some other quarter.[5]

In this situation of adversity the reality of a subsistence penal colony was fully realized.

It is not the intention here to explore fully the relationship between the motivation for the choice of Botany Bay, and the functioning of the colony in its early years. The writer has dealt with aspects of this topic elsewhere, and hopes to develop the theme in another volume. The purpose of this chapter is to suggest that the government's limited conception of the function of New South Wales remained unaltered down to the Peace of Amiens, and that ministers could not be awakened to the potential strategic or commercial value of the colony. Even when the governors and some of the local inhabitants of New South Wales began to point towards a more balanced development, Pitt and his fellow ministers remained unimpressed. Pleas for properly trained farmers and fewer unskilled convicts to be sent out were also ignored. Only when it was finally realized that efforts to create a self-sufficient, communal subsistence economy were impractical, and were resulting in increases to the financial burden on the metropolitan government, was consideration given to moving the penal colony in other directions. The principal concern of the ministry once the colony was established was keeping the costs as low as possible to forestall criticisms in England. So preoccupied was the government with this aspect that one governor was recalled because of the spiralling increase in bills drawn on London.

The original hope of the ministry was that New South Wales would be self-sufficient in food within two years of the fleet sailing. Initially all agricultural work was to be carried out on government farms by supervised gangs of convicts. As sentences ran their course, or convicts were emancipated, small land grants would be made and the new farmers would practise a form of peasant farming, supporting their families and perhaps contributing a little towards the public stock. With their small surpluses these peasants would be able to purchase the limited quantity of hardware, implements and clothing that would be needed.[6] In the first five years it proved difficult to fulfil these objectives as poor equipment, lack of convicts with agricultural experience, poor seed, droughts and poor soils restricted development.[7] Not until settlement spread to the fertile banks of the Hawkesbury did the colony begin to produce grain and vegetables in useful quantities. Occasional heavy flooding could destroy even this slender lifeline.

After Governor Phillip's departure at the end of 1792, the Acting Governor, Francis Grose, began making large land grants, mostly to the serving and retired officers.[8] This practice was continued by his successor and initially this led to a substantial increase in grain production. Eventually these larger farmers turned towards pastoralism, leaving the smallholders as the main arable farmers.[9] As this policy became entrenched the government farms, deprived of their necessary labour, went into decline. In the period of Hunter's governorship, there were sometimes large surpluses of maize and wheat and because of the absence of an export market, these supplies were all received by the commissariat, which drew bills on the Treasury to pay for the purchases.[10] Towards the end of the 1790s the costs of the colony began to rise alarmingly and Secretary of State Portland issued demands for restraint. In departing from their instructions governors had moved away from the subsistence farming model mapped out when the colony was first planned. Since the departure of Phillip the public farms had been run down and the convicts who had worked them were extravagantly supplied to the officers and settlers, while being maintained from the store. The prices paid for grain and pork had been inflated, labour costs were too high and disreputable forms of currency were in circulation. To rectify this situation the government farms were to be built up again, large farmers were to feed and clothe those they employed and all non-assigned felons were to be employed in the way most conducive to their own subsistence without regard for the effect this might have on the value of the private farmers' produce.[11] In December 1798 he described for Hunter's benefit the model economy for New South Wales: government farms operating side by side with those of the smallholders, both producing just enough to feed the labourers which they employed. The large landowners were patently an embarrassment to the ministry. It is clear that Portland's conception of the function and functioning of the colony was the same as that of his predecessors in office. New South Wales was to be a cheap, isolated penal colony which would largely finance itself and not intrude its problems on the government, which had weightier matters to deal with.

The attitude of the home government was also evident in the failure to respond to suggestions from New South Wales that the colony should develop in other directions, or had a future other than as a penal colony. When the first fleet sailed the decision was taken not to send out further convicts until favourable reports of the new colony reached England. As has been shown, this placed considerable strain on the hulks and jails in the interim, but the government did not wish to face a fiasco on the scale of the West African experiment in the last war. During this interval the Home Office acknowledged the possibility that the New South Wales scheme might have to be abandoned and therefore it developed contingency plans for sending further shipments of convicts elsewhere. In late October 1788 Sydney suggested to the Treasury that if reports from New South Wales proved unfavourable a North American site would be chosen instead. The alternative site was Nova Scotia, and the next shipload of convicts to be transported wàs ready to be re-routed to that destination if necessary.[12] If the New South Wales gamble failed the project would be abandoned and the Nova Scotians would be pressed into accepting convicts. As far as the ministry was concerned, unless the colony could perform its primary function as a penal colony, it was of limited utility. All references to other possible uses for New South Wales were forgotten at this stage.

Only the barest assurances of the survivability of New South Wales were necessary before the ministry despatched more convicts. The earliest news from the colony, received in England in 1789, can have given little more than a preliminary report, and no information about the real state of agriculture. It seemed enough that the convicts had survived the voyage out, and had not been slaughtered or swept by fever on arrival. The ministry nonetheless made plain its rather fickle attachment to the chosen site of the penal settlement in the first despatch of William Grenville, who had replaced the slothful Sydney in June 1789. Responding to Phillip's comments on the quality of the soil at Port Jackson and the hostility of the Aborigines, Grenville expressed the view that Norfolk Island was the 'most favorable position', because of the luxuriant soil and lack of any indigenous inhabitants. He went on: 'and were it not for the great labour and expence incurred already at Port Jackson, I should have been inclined to have recommended that island's being the principal settlement . . .'. It was fully realized at this time that there was no harbour or shelter for ships at Norfolk Island and therefore strategic thoughts were far from Grenville's mind. He nevertheless urged that the establishment there be augmented, and if similar spots were discovered they too should be settled. If Frost's assumption is correct, the views of Grenville can be regarded as synonymous with those of the Prime Minister.[13]

From the government point of view, the questions of cost and convenience were uppermost, and fertile soils meant early self-sufficiency; absence of indigenous people meant low defence costs. Ironically, the original reason for settling Norfolk Island was to prevent an occupation by any other power, as this would have left Botany Bay vulnerable. In its confusion, the government believed the island was closer to the mainland than it actually was.[14] Obviously, the attachment to New South Wales itself was precarious, and altogether unrelated to wider questions of imperial purpose.

For this reason the government had no further uses for the smokescreens of hemp and flax after 1788: indeed these would become positive liabilities once the Opposition or persons outside government began to demand that words be supported by action. Apart from the request from Brook Watson for New Zealand flax seeds, the Pitt ministry avoided any mention of the subject of raising or processing flax in Australasia. This complete indifference contrasted sharply with the great enthusiasm shown by Governor Phillip, and Lieutenant-Governor King on Norfolk Island. Credulous men that they were, they had taken the references to flax in their instructions seriously, and without the proper equipment, or resources, or even trained men, they had doggedly set about trying to harvest and process the product.

Why was there such enthusiasm at the periphery of the empire for a project which was now deliberately ignored in England? There was a reason other than naivety and enthusiasm for the actions of Phillip and King. Although in the view of government they had been sent out to guard England's criminal wastes, in their own eyes they were founding a new dominion. Predictably, they did not wish to be seen as little more than prison keepers, but wanted to become true colonial governors with all the prestige and perquisites which that entailed. For this reason they took it as axiomatic that the penal phase in New South Wales would be a short one, and that with the arrival of free settlers and the development of an export industry, the colony would begin to look more like a traditional component of empire.[15] Their need for a colonial staple was therefore a personal and colonial necessity, rather than a strategic one. This explained the sometimes frenetic efforts of New South Wales governors to find and promote export commodities. Sealing and whaling, coal and, eventually wool attracted their attention. However in the early days of the colony a flax industry was the only one which sprang to mind.

And so for the first decade in Norfolk Island, and even in New South Wales itself, these agents of empire turned their attention to flax culture. Phillip, confused by his Instructions, searched for the plant in New South Wales, but could only find the flax lily *Doryanthus excelsa* and the native flax *Gymnostachys anceps*. Both of these were rather wiry and sparse for any manufacturing purposes.[16] King was a little more fortunate. He found the New Zealand flax *Phormium tenax* around the shores of Norfolk Island and, following his instructions from Phillip to the letter, he set convicts to work processing it. Despite his dedication and energy, the work of the convicts employed on this task was slow, and King and Phillip pressed the home government for proper equipment and trained men.[17] By the beginning of 1791 there was a man on Norfolk Island who claimed some knowledge of flax dressing and in February he had managed to produce two pieces of coarse cloth, one of which was sent to

Phillip in Sydney. Towards the end of the year he had graduated to coarse canvas. Problems in dressing the flax were still formidable and the output was low and uneven in quality. For this reason in 1793 King resorted to the desperate expedient of kidnapping two Maoris from New Zealand to instruct the convicts in flax dressing. Unfortunately information about the Maori economy was then limited, and the two men taken to Norfolk Island proved of little use. It was the women who dressed flax in their society.

While Lieutenant-Governor Grose and Governor Hunter largely abandoned efforts to produce flax goods, King continued his interest until his return to England in 1796. The reason for this was his great faith in the future of Norfolk Island, and the encouragement he received from Sir Joseph Banks.[18] There was certainly no encouragement from the government. Flax, and the difficulties in cultivating and working it, featured in countless despatches from New South Wales and Norfolk Island, but these references were studiously ignored at Westminster. The requests for trained men and proper equipment fell on deaf ears. Initially crestfallen, the enthusiasts in New South Wales and Norfolk Island eventually became resigned to the official attitude in London. Even the resolution of Lieutenant-Governor King faltered when confronted with an example of industry so blatantly unrewarded.

Pitt and his colleagues seemed equally oblivious of any continuing or potential strategic role for New South Wales, although as the years went by it did create its own strategic necessities. The garrison at Port Jackson remained under strength and inadequate for its primary purposes before the Peace of Amiens. Because of internal squabbles and their general lack of cooperation, the Marine Corps had to be withdrawn and replaced with the specially raised New South Wales Corps under Francis Grose. The numbers in this corps failed to keep pace with the increase in the convict population, and because of the need for detached duty at such places as Norfolk Island, Parramatta and the Hawkesbury, its resources were always perilously stretched. This was evident in the difficulty in finding sufficient officers to serve on General Courts Martial, or even the Criminal Court. As settlement pushed out to areas like the Hawkesbury and confrontation with the Aboriginal population increased, the Corps was dangerously dispersed and weakened. In the war years it would not have been able to mount effective resistance against outside attack.

Governors and commanders of the Corps requested that its numbers be augmented, but the government was preoccupied with the war in Europe and ignored all such pleas. After 1802 the size of the garrison was actually reduced by the Secretary of State, in spite of the danger of convict rebellions. The same indifference which prompted that action is evident in the matter of artillery. The inhabitants of Sydney were acutely aware of their vulnerability to attack from the sea, and governors persistently sought to increase the size of the battery and recruit skilled artillery officers. In 1802 Governor King appointed the convicted murderer George Bellasis to take charge of the battery, so desperate was he for men of experience. Repeated requests to London for men and artillery were ignored.

In naval terms also the settlement was weak. From the outset, the ministry had shown no intention of stationing warships in New South Wales, or in developing facilities where naval vessels could refit. As has been shown, the initial plan was that the armed storeship *Sirius* should be withdrawn once the colony was reasonably secure, and Phillip's instructions requested him to send her home at such a time.[19] The cost of maintaining the *Sirius* on the service was calculated at £31 663 over a three-year period and her withdrawal would produce therefore a net reduction in the financial burden of the colony. In the event this proved unnecessary—the dilapidated vessel ran on to the rocks at Norfolk Island in March 1790.[20]

At the time of this misfortune the ship still had a vital function to perform in transporting supplies from the Cape of Good Hope. As a replacement Phillip used the Dutch vessel *Waaksamheyd* of 300 tons, which had been hired at Batavia in July 1790 to carry stores to Port Jackson. In his despatch of February 1791, Grenville expressed the hope that this bluff-bowed storeship, together with the *Supply* would be adequate for the future purposes of the colony.[21] Clearly he saw no military role for these vessels. In 1791 the *Waaksamheyd* sailed for England with Captain Hunter and the crew of the *Sirius* on board, and the government saw no urgent need to replace it. Eventually, the *Porpoise* was sent out, but like her predecessor she was a storeship and not a man of war: she had no strategic capacity whatsoever.

In the years from 1788 to the Peace of Amiens the government did not include New South Wales in an imperial strategy, least of all one geared to the defence of India. It has been suggested that the draft plans to use New South Wales as a recruitment centre during the Nootka Sound crisis testified to the imperial vision and span of the Pitt ministry, and their foresight in the settlement of New South Wales.[22] This suggestion is unlikely. Before the sailing of the first fleet there was no indication that the ministry foresaw a role for the colony in relation to the north-west coast of America. It was envisaged that certain supplies for Botany Bay could be obtained at the Spice Islands and the Pacific, and that Polynesian women might be imported from the Pacific to balance the sex ratios in the new colonial society, thereby maintaining morality. However the government manifested no territorial ambitions towards the north-west coast of America, and had been at best luke-warm to the fur traders who were interested in the area.[23]

The Spanish seizure of vessels in Nootka Sound on Vancouver

Island in 1789 could not have been predicted, but it required a response. When news of the seizure reached London in February 1790, the ministry was caught unawares, but a show of force was planned to meet the threat. The storeship *Gorgon* was about to depart for Port Jackson. She was hastily prepared for a longer voyage to Nootka Sound. With her went the sloop *Discovery*, which at that time was about to embark on a surveying voyage to the south Atlantic. These two were to be joined by a frigate from the East India squadron which was to rendezvous with the other vessels in the Sandwich Islands. On the way to Hawaii the *Gorgon* and *Discovery* were to pick up a small party which would form the basis of a settlement at the reclaimed territory on Vancouver Island. Instructions setting up this mission were hurriedly despatched to Commodore Cornwallis in India and to Governor Phillip at Port Jackson. Captain Vancouver's expedition later sailed to receive back the appropriated land at Nootka Sound, and to survey the north-west coast of America.[24]

It is obvious that this punitive expedition was put together in great haste with the men and materials most readily available. It was very much a piecemeal and ramshackle enterprise, and it was perhaps fortunate that an accommodation was worked out with Spain before the ships actually put to sea. Although New South Wales featured in the plans, it was as a way station, and as an obvious place to collect convict settlers. There was no suggestion that the expedition could not have been mounted without recourse to the settlement. After all, the settlers could have been loaded in England or even in India, and Cook's ships had found Queen Charlotte and Dusky Sounds and Tahiti perfectly satisfactory as refreshment stops.

In the war years New South Wales did not feature in the naval strategy concerning the defence of India and the sea lanes to China. No warships called at the port to refresh, and no strategic supplies were shipped from there to bases in India or south-east Asia. As has been shown, there were no attempts to build up the defences of Port Jackson, or its ordnance supplies. Predictably, the British response to the French and Dutch threats in the East was a frontal rather than a flanking one. The French base at Pondicherry fell very quickly in 1793, the Cape in 1795; Malacca and Trincomalee in the same year. While attacks on the Île de France failed before 1808, Colombo, Amboina and other Dutch possessions were in British hands by 1796. The aim was not to find a way around French and Dutch power in the East but to destroy it. New South Wales was not called upon to play a part in the deployment of ships and men for the defence of eastern seas. In spite of French privateering depredations from Île de France and Bourbon, it was not considered worthwhile sending the China fleet by way of Port Jackson: it was too distant, and the routes north of the colony were not sufficiently well known. The answer to the privateering threat to East India Company ships was the convoy system as it always had been.[25]

Far from supporting the defence of the Indian empire, New South Wales became partially dependent upon it for its own survival. In September 1790 Grenville had suggested to Governor General Cornwallis that certain provisions for New South Wales might be procured at Calcutta at lower prices than they could in England, thereby reducing the burden on government. He intended that a supply ship should make the journey from Port Jackson to collect the provisions.[26] In October 1791 the storeship *Atlantic* was sent to Calcutta under Lieutenant Bowen, and a cargo of basic provisions was collected.[27] This marked the beginning of a regular but one-way connection between Bengal and New South Wales. At several points during the war years the timely arrival of a cargo from Calcutta averted disaster at Port Jackson.

Of course once the colony was established it created its own limited strategic necessities. Although it could offer no support to a wider imperial strategy, and had not been founded for this purpose, it needed a modicum of protection itself, as did the sea routes to it. As has been suggested already, the orders to occupy Norfolk Island had this motive behind them. In Phillip's Instructions the reasons for establishing a settlement were 'to secure the same to us, and prevent it being occupied by the subjects of any other European power'.[28] The French explorer La Perouse was known to be in the Pacific at this time, and French possession of an island off the New South Wales coast might expose Port Jackson to depredatory raids in a wartime situation. Of course it was soon discovered that Norfolk Island had no harbour and consequently was quite useless from a naval viewpoint.

The same principle was apparent in respect of the Baudin expedition in 1800 and 1801. His voyage offered no threat to the Indian empire, but his interest in the western and southern coasts of New Holland created nervousness about the sea approaches to Port Jackson. The sailing of Baudin was one of the factors inspiring the Flinders expedition, and news of the Frenchman's activities around Bass Strait and Van Dieman's Land was an obvious element in the decision to found settlements at Port Phillip, the Derwent and Port Dalrymple. But even in these instances the behaviour of the British government was reactive in nature, rather than the result of long-term planning. Far from 'increasing the nation's strategic capacity in the East', the foundation of New South Wales had only added to Britain's strategic burdens.

Chapter 9

CONCLUSION

In the four decades after the Seven Years' War, British mariners had performed a remarkable task in opening up the Pacific. The new age of discovery attained its highest technical and geographical achievement in the three voyages of Captain James Cook. With their scientific personnel and equipment, masterly examples of navigation and seamanship, and their attention to detail, these voyages established a tradition, and also a model of discovery. They served to set the standards for subsequent Pacific voyages by men such as Bligh, Vancouver, Broughton and Flinders.

It is of course tempting to portray these voyages as part of a sustained and coordinated British assault on the Pacific: as elements in what V.T. Harlow described as a 'swing to the east' in British imperial policy.[1] The annexation of New South Wales in January 1788 can, and has been, placed within this framework, and thus been viewed as merely a facet of a concentrated British assault on the Pacific.

When viewed from this rather deterministic perspective the settlement of New South Wales becomes an almost inevitable element of imperial expansion in the region. The questions of intention and motivation become self-evident and self-explanatory, and are outlined in terms of imperial concomitants of trade and naval power. This view assumes the determined intervention by politicians and officials of vision, eager to expand commercial opportunities and forms of territorial dominion. This interpretation has a logic of its own, which is based on faith in the ability of people to set desirable goals and pursue them successfully. It leaves little room for randomness, expediency or incompetence in the management of affairs. In the context of a question such as the settlement of New South Wales, such an overview serves to depress the importance of what are seen as subsidiary domestic matters—such as the convict crisis.

However, the argument has been that New South Wales cannot be fitted into this broader pattern of imperial expansion. Attempts to do so have distorted our record of the past, and sought to create a myth of a better national origin. They have also overestimated the capacity of governments in the late eighteenth century.

Although some merchants and speculators were eager to exploit the discoveries of Captain Cook, British governments after 1780 were slow to realize the implications and potential of his voyages, much less integrate them into a new imperial vision. Successive governments were badly placed and too poorly equipped to give a lead to commercial endeavour.

There was, by contrast, much that was haphazard and *ad hoc* about British administration in this period, and the decision to send convicts to Botany Bay fits into this pattern of expediency. It was not a carefully premeditated decision nestling within the confines of a coherent imperial policy. It was a desperate step, taken in confusion; clutching at an unsuitable last resort. Once taken, the decision was implemented in a shoddy way. The new outpost of empire was scarcely able to survive with the scant human and material resources it had been given. It was incapable of fulfilling any wider or more profound imperial aspirations. Expectations based on the glowing descriptions in promotional literature were soon replaced with despondency, and a sense of having been abandoned. From such inauspicious beginnings Australia grew to maturity and nationhood.

NOTES

1 INTRODUCTION

1 Blagden to Banks, 17 September 1786, B.M. (N.H.), D.T.C. 5, f. 58.
2 Dalrymple to Court of Directors, 13 May 1785, N.L. Dalrymple MS 43/4. Memorandum on Convicts, 1 September 1786, *ibid.*, 43/5.
3 Report of the Beauchamp Committee, 21 June 1785, H.O. 28/6, f. 257.
4 Alan Frost, *Convicts and Empire. A Naval Question*, pp. xiv–xv, 121.
5 K.M. Dallas, 'The first settlements in Australia: considered in relation to sea-power in world politics', in Ged Martin (ed.), *The Founding of Australia*, p. 49. K.M. Dallas, *Trading Posts or Penal Colonies. Cook's Route to Pacific Trade*, p. 2. Michael Roe, 'Australia's place in the "swing to the East" 1788–1810', *ibid.*, pp. 60–1. O.H.K. Spate, in *Historical Studies*, vol. 19, no. 76, April 1981, p. 458. Frost, *op. cit.*, pp. 182, 135.
6 Russel Ward, *The Australian Legend*, p. 21.
7 Michael Roe, 'Challenges to Australian Identity', *Quadrant*, no. 129, vol. XXII, no. 4, April 1978, p. 34.
8 There are of course notable exceptions to this pattern, the most distinguished being the first volume of Manning Clark's *A History of Australia*. There has also been valuable work on convict society such as A.G.L. Shaw, *Convicts and Colonies*, and L.L. Robson, *The Convict Settlers of Australia*. The most recent contribution in this area is J.B. Hirst, *Convict Society and its Enemies. A History of Early New South Wales*. Recent examples of the tendency to rush through this early period in general works are: A.F. Madden and W.H. Morris Jones (eds), *Australia and Britain. Studies in a Changing Relationship*; W.G. McMinn, *A Constitutional History of Australia*; G.J.R. Linge, *Industrial Awakening. A Geography of Australian Manufacturing, 1788–1890*; Henry Reynolds (ed.), *Aborigines and Settlers, the Australian Experience, 1788–1939*.
9 This emphasis is apparent in a number of works of economic history: G.J. Abbott and N.B. Nairn (eds), *Economic Growth of Australia, 1788–1833*; D.R. Hainsworth, *Builders and Adventurers: The Traders and the Emergence of the Colony*; and *The Sydney Traders. Simeon Lord and his Contemporaries*; Margaret Steven, *Merchant Campbell, 1764–1846. A Study in Colonial Trade*; G. Dow, *Samuel Terry, the Botany Bay Rothschild*.

10 N.B. Nairn, in Abbott and Nairn, *op. cit.*, p. 55.
11 Frost, *op. cit.*, p. 160.
12 Margaret Stevens, *Trade, Tactics and Territory. Britain in the Pacific, 1783–1823*, p. 116.
13 A point I have developed in more detail elsewhere: see D.L. Mackay, 'Direction and Purpose in British Imperial Policy, 1783–1801', *Historical Journal*, vol. XVII, 3(1974), pp. 487–501.

2   THE CONVICT CRISIS 1775–90

1   39 Eliz., cap 64.
2   M. Ignatieff, *A Just Measure of Pain*, p. 20.
3   Ignatieff, *op. cit.*, p. 15. J.M. Beattie, 'Crime and the Courts in Surrey 1736–1753', in J.S. Cockburn (ed.), *Crime in England, 1550–1800*.
4   Beattie, *op. cit.*, p. 162.
5   Ignatieff, *op. cit.*, p. 28. Joanna Innes, 'The King's Bench Prison in the Later Eighteenth Century', in J. Brewer and J. Styles (eds), *An Ungovernable People*, pp. 250–98.
6   Douglas Hay, 'Property, Authority and the Criminal Law', in D. Hay, P. Linebaugh and E.P. Thompson (eds), *Albion's Fatal Tree*, p. 51.
7   M. Radzinowicz, *A History of the Criminal Law in England*, vol. 1, pp. 147, 150–2.
8   J. Beattie, *op. cit.*, p. 180.
9   J. Cobley, *The Crimes of the First Fleet Convicts*.
10 Grenville to Phillip, 19 February 1791, C.O. 201/5, 62.
11 Petition of Leicester prisoners, 20 July 1785, H.O. 42/7, 315.
12 A.G.L. Shaw, *Convicts and Colonies*, p. 34.
13 The Hulks Act, 16 Geo. III. c. 43.
14 W. Branch-Johnson, *The English Prison Hulks*, p. 18.
15 Ignatieff, *op. cit.*, p. 81.
16 Minutes of the Beauchamp Committee, 26 March 1785, H.O. 7/1.
17 Ignatieff, *op. cit.*, p. 81.
18 B.R. Mitchell, *Abstract of British Historical Statistics*, pp. 346, 497–8.
19 J. Fortescue (ed.), *The Correspondence of George the Third*, vol. VI, p. 386. D. Hay, 'War, Dearth and Theft in the Eighteenth Century', *Past & Present*, vol. 95, May 1982, pp. 139–40.
20 T.S. Ashton, *An Economic History of England. The Eighteenth Century*, pp. 250, 254.
21 Hay, 'War, Dearth and Theft', *op. cit.*, pp. 140–3, 145.
22 John Beattie, 'The Pattern of Crime in England 1660-1800', *Past & Present*, vol. 62, February 1974, pp. 74–7, 91.
23 Townshend to Newcastle, 23 October 1782, H.O. 43/1, 45.
24 Ignatieff, *op. cit.*, p. 87.
25 M. Blaug, 'The Myth of the Old Poor Law and the Making of the New', *Journal of Economic History*, XXIII,(1963), p. 153. Ignatieff, op. cit., p. 84.
26 An example of the local reaction is in John Money, *Experience and Identity. Birmingham and the West Midlands, 1760–1800*, p. 14. On Pitt's financial measures, see John Ehrman, *The Younger Pitt*, ch. X.

27   Ignatieff, *op. cit.*, p. 84. Ackerman testimony to Beauchamp Committee, 26 March 1785, H.O. 7/1. The prison had been rebuilt in 1767, but without any great increase in its capacity.
28   Sydney to Lords of Adm., November 1785, H.O. 28/5, 143.
29   John Beattie, in Cockburn, *op. cit.*, p. 162.
30   These figures come from the Home Office, Domestic Papers in H.O. 42/5-9.
31   Ignatieff, *op. cit.*, p. 85. H.O. 47/1, 9 February 1784.
32   H.O. 42/4, 19 January 1784. H.O. 42/5, September 1784.
33   E.A.L. Moir, 'Sir George Onesiphorous Paul', in H.P.R. Finberg (ed.), *Gloucestershire Studies*, p. 204.
34   W.J. Sheehan, 'Finding Solace in Eighteenth Century Newgate', in Cockburn, *op. cit.*, p. 230. P. Linebaugh, 'The Ordinary of Newgate and his Account', *ibid.*, p. 257.
35   Quoted in Frost, *op. cit.*, p. 9.
36   Sydney to Lords of Adm., l9 March 1787, H.O. 29/2, 103. Phillip to Sydney, 2 September 1787, C.O. 201/2, 180.
37   These figures are taken from the Home Office, Domestic papers, H.O. 42/5-9.
38   W. Branch-Johnson, *The English Prison Hulks*, p. 11.
39   Lord Mayor to Nepean, 21 November 1984, H.O. 32/1.
40   Branch-Johnson, *op. cit.*, p. 15.
41   Branch-Johnson, *op. cit.*, p. 10.
42   Ignatieff, *op. cit.*, p. 85. H.O. 42/5, 373, 14 December 1784. H.O. 42/9, 313, 10 August 1786.
43   Petition of Prisoners, 20 July 1785, H.O. 42/7, 315.
44   Sydney to Lords of Adm., 29 May 1784, H.O. 28/4, 143. ADM. 2/260, 161.
45   Sydney to Mayor of Hull, 9 December 1784, H.O. 43/1, 351.
46   Sydney to Spencer, 18 December 1784, H.O. 42/5, 375.
47   Treasury papers, T. 1/614, 9 January 1785. H.O. 35/1, 9 February 1785.
48   Sydney to Lords of Treasury, 10 November 1785, H.O. 35/6.
49   See below, Chapter 4.
50   I.R. Christie, *Wars and Revolutions*. Britain 1760–1815, pp. 198-204.
51   L. Namier and J. Brooke, *The History of Parliament 1754–1790*, vol. 2, pp. 64-5; vol. 3, p. 373.
52   Rolle to Nepean, 5 May 1786, H.O. 42/8, 2O8.
53   Pitt to Rolle, 6 May 1786, P.R.O. Chatham papers, 30/8/195, 31.
54   *c.f.* Frost, *op. cit.*, p. 110.
55   Rolle to Townshend, 7 May 1786, H.O. 42/8, 214. Contractors to Nepean, 6 May 1786, *ibid.*, 212.
56   Nepean to Steele, 10 June 1786, T. 1/632.
57   Steele to Nepean, 29 October 1787, H.O. 35/8.
58   W. Richards to Treasury, 13 October 1788, H.O. 35/9.
59   H.O. 29/2, 85, 24 May 1788. Sydney to Adm. Lords, 14 May 1787, *ibid.*, 29/2, 115.
60   Sydney to Treasury Lords, 31 October 1789, H.O. 35/9.
61   Mullender to Nepean, 6 May 1789, H.O. 42/14, 56. Grenville to Lowther, 8 September 1789, H.O. 42/15, 182-3.

62   Sydney to Lord Chief Justice Clerk, 22 February 1787, H.O. 103/1, 72–4. Scottish Lord Advocate to Sydney, 12 October 1787, H.O. 102/51, 179–181. Lord Provost and Magistrates of Glasgow to Sydney, 31 January 1788, ibid., 203. Magistrates of Aberdeen to Sydney, 28 April 1788, *ibid.*, 242–8.

63   Richards to Keeper Brecon jail, 5 February 1789, H.O. 42/4, 132–3.

64   H.O. 42/15, 268, 7 October 1789. C. Wareham to Nepean, 14 October 1789, *ibid.*, 296.

65   Lumby to Banks, 21 November 1789 and 13 November 1790, M.L. Yale FM4, 4365.

3 PRIVATE ENTERPRISE AND THE SOUTHERN OCEANS

1   These are discussed in, D.L. Mackay, 'Exploration and the Economic Development of Empire, 1782–1798', University of London Ph.D. thesis, 1970.

2   A Rainaud, *Le Continent Austral*.

3   N.L. Petherick MSS 760/17/342.

4   A Dalrymple, *A Collection of Voyages Chiefly in the Southern Atlantick Ocean*, p. 6.

5   J.C. Beaglehole (ed.), *The Journals of Captain Cook on His Voyages of Discovery*, vol. II, p. 688.

6   Beaglehole, *op. cit.*, vol. III, p. lxxii. Vancouver to Banks, n.d., B.M. (N.H.), D.T.C. V, pp. 228–9.

7   On the 1783 voyage, see below, Chapter 6.

8   Matra to Banks, 28 July 1783, Add. MSS 33977, 206.

9   Banks to Atkinson, 15 January 1782, M.L. FM4, 4363. Banks to Grigsby, 1 June 1782, *ibid.*

10   Matra to North, 23 August 1783, C.O. 201/1, 57–61, with covering letters, 62–4.

11   Frost, *op. cit.*, p. 12.

12   *Ibid.*, p. 15.

13   Matra memorandum in G. Martin, *The Founding of Australia*, p. 15–16.

14   Matra to Nepean, 1 November 1784, in Martin, *op. cit.*, p. 17, with enclosures.

15   See below, Chapter 4.

16   These proposals are described in Frost, *op. cit.*, pp. 16–19.

17   Evidence before the Beauchamp Committee, 2 May 1785, H.O. 7/1. Thompson to Nepean, 24 April 1785, H.O. 42/6, 335.

18   Alexander Davison to Nepean, 3 February 1793, C.O. 201/8, 148–9, enclosing Young's letter.

19   Young Plan, C.O. 201/1, 51–4, with printed copy at 55-6. A. Atkinson, 'Whigs and Tories and Botany Bay', *Journal of the Royal Australian Historical Society*, vol. 61, March 1975, pp. 295–6.

20   *Ibid.*, p. 296.

21   Frost, *op. cit.*, pp. 19–24, gives details of these schemes.

22   Evidence to Beauchamp Committee, 28 April 1785. H.O. 7/1.

23   Young and Call plan, 24 May 1788, C.O. 201/3, 171.

24   These various proposals are in H.O. 42/7, 23–56.

25   Frost, *op. cit.*, p. 24–6, 203, n. 13.

26 Reports dated December 1784, in H.O. 42/5, 411–3.
27 Howe to Sydney, 26 December 1784, H.O. 28/4, 386.
28 Arden to Sydney, 13 January 1785, C.O. 201/1, 51.
29 Young and Call plan, 21 June 1785, I.O. E/1/76, 213. Dalrymple memorandum, 13 July 1785. N.L. Dalrymple MS 43/4.
30 Brook Watson to Board of Trade, 13 October 1789, B.T. 5/5, 192.
31 The scheme is in W. Devaynes to Dundas, 17 September 1785, S.R.O. *Melville* MSS G.D. 51/3/17, 1. D. Dalrymple to Devaynes, 17 September 1785, *ibid.*, 2. Pitt to Grenville, 2 October 1785, H.M.C. *Dropmore*, no. 30, pt. 1, p. 157. See also Mollie Gillen, 'The Botany Bay Decision, 1786: convicts not empire', *English Historical Review*, vol. XCVII, no. 385, October 1782, p. 753.
32 Frost, *op. cit.*, p. 98.
33 Blankett to Nepean, 10 August 1786, H.O. 42/9, 323.
34 Blankett to Nepean, *ibid.*
35 Frost, *op. cit.*, p. 119. Frost takes his subtitle 'A Naval Question' from Blankett's letter.
36 Dalrymple to E.I.C. Directors, 1 September 1786, N.L. Dalrymple MS. 43/5.
37 Blankett to Nepean, November 1786, H.O. 42/10, 418–22.
38 Petition of Young and Call, 25 May 1788, C.O. 201/3, 171. Phillip's Instructions are in C.O. 202/5, 28–38, 24 April 1787.
39 Blankett to Nepean, 4 June 1789, H.O. 42/14, 172.
40 Alexander Davison to Nepean, 12 February 1793, C.O. 201/8, 146–9, enc. Young to Davison, 3 February 1793.

4   GOVERNMENT PLANS FOR THE DISPOSAL OF CONVICTS

1 G. Martin, 'The Founding of Botany Bay', in Hyam and Martin, *op. cit.*, pp. 49, 52-7. Gillen, *op. cit.*
2 *Ibid.*, p. 49.
3 Martin, *op. cit.*, p. 49. Nepean evidence before Beauchamp Committee, 27 April 1785, H.O. 7/1.
4 A.G.L. Shaw, *Convicts and Colonies*, pp. 42-3. Gillen, *op. cit.*, p. 743.
5 *Commons Journal*, XXXVII, 306-313. Frost, op. cit., p. 7.
6 *Commons Journal*, XXVII, 310-13.
7 *Ibid.*
8 H.O. 42/6, 381. H.O. 42/5, 390–3.
9 Gillen, *op. cit.*, p. 746.
10 North to George III, 11 July 1783, J. Fortescue, *The Correspondence of George the Third*, vol. IV, pp. 415–6.
11 The details of this fiasco come from reports of the trials in J.S. Cobley, *Crimes of the First Fleet Convicts*, pp. xi, xii. A.G.L. Shaw, *Convicts and Colonies*, p. 45. Fortescue, *op. cit*, vol. VI, pp. 415–16, 418, 440.
12 Cobley, *op. cit.*, p. xiii.
13 J.A. Burdon, *The Archives of British Honduras*, vol. 1, pp. 146–7.
14 These details come from, Cobley, *op. cit.*, pp. xi-xii. G. Martin, 'The Founding of Botany Bay', in Hyam and Martin, *op. cit.*, pp. 50-3.

15   V.T. Harlow, *The Founding of the Second British Empire*, vol. I, pp. 343-4, 354, 359. Fortescue, *op. cit.*, pp. 194–6.
16   Burdon, *op. cit.*, p. 149.
17   de Freire to Nepean, 17 November 1784, H.O. 42/5, 323.
18   These plans are in H.O. 42/5, December 1784. Frost, *op. cit.*, pp. 93-4.
19   Sydney to Africa Committee, 14 December 1784, H.O. 43/1, 353. Sydney to Gilbert Ross, 21 December 1784, *ibid.*, 355.
20   H.O. 42/4, 411.
21   Howe to Sydney, 26 December 1784, H.O. 28/4, 386.
22   Frost, *op. cit.*, p. 93.
23   Gillen, *op. cit.*, p.748.
24   On the peace negotiations and their outcome, see Harlow *op. cit.*, vol. 1, ch. 7. H.A. Gailey, *A History of the Gambia*, pp. 33–4. J.M. Gray, *History of the Gambia*, pp. 272-80. E.C. Martin, *The British West Africa Settlements, 1750–1821*, pp. 99–102.
25   Gray, *op. cit.*, pp. 273–4.
26   Lords of Adm. to Sydney, 28 July 1784, H.O. 28/4, 209. H.O. 28/5, 1, 5 January 1785.
27   Gray, *op. cit.*, p. 277.
28   Frost, *op. cit.*, p. 29. Beauchamp Committee Minutes, H.O. 7/1. Roberts to Ross, December 1784, H.O. 42/5, 390–3. Barnes to Nepean, 3 January 1785, H.O. 42/6, 8.
29   Gray, *op. cit.*, p. 278.
30   Sydney to Lords of Treasury, 9 February 1785, H.O. 35/1. Barnes to Nepean, 13 January 1785, H.O. 42/6, 25.
31   Sydney to Lords of Treasury, *op. cit.*, enclosure 1. Gillen, *op. cit.*, p. 749.
32   *Ibid.*, enclosures.
33   Frost, *op. cit.*, p. 32.
34   T. 1/616, 28 February 1785.
35   Frost, *op. cit.*, p. 32.
36   Frost, *op. cit.*, pp. 34-5. Gillen, *op. cit.*, p. 750.
37   For Nepean's evidence see the Minutes of the Beauchamp Committee, H.O. 7/1.
38   First Report in H.O. 42/6, 373-382, 9 May 1785.
39   See Frost, *op. cit.*, p. 37.
40   Report of Beauchamp Committee in, H.O. 47/7, 3. This written reply was in answer to a Committee request for plans.
41   Gillen, *op. cit.*, p. 750.
42   Testimony of 9 May 1785, in H.O. 7/1.
43   *Ibid.*, 12 May 1785.
44   Campbell to Nepean, 22 January 1786, H.O. 42/8, 43.
45   J. Ehrman, *The Younger Pitt*, p. 52
46   *Ibid.*, p. 157. I.R. Christie, *Wars and Revolutions*, pp. 184–8.
47   John Rolle and John Pollexfen Bastard; see above Chapter 2.
48   Lorien Reid, *Charles James Fox*, p. 216.
49   Frost, *op. cit.*, p. 34. Gillen, *op. cit.*, p. 751.
50   Nepean note, H.O. 42/1, 462.
51   Frost, *op. cit.*, p. 46.
52   Frost, *op. cit.*, p. 41.

53 Beauchamp Committee Report, 21 June 1785, H.O. 42/6, 463.
54 H.O. 28/5, 116, 16 August 1785.
55 H.O. 28/5, 118, 22 August 1785.
56 H.O. 28/4, 209, 28 July 1784. H.O. 28/5, 1, 13, 15, 43, 5 January, 7 February, 9 February, 5 March 1785. H.O. 28/61, 36, 24 August 1785.
57 Details of this voyage and its preparations are in D. Mackay, 'British Interest in the Southern Oceans, 1783–1801', *New Zealand Journal of History*, vol. 3, no. 2, October 1969, pp. 124–42.
58 H.O. 35/6, 10 November 1785.
59 T. 1/614, 9 November 1785.
60 H.O. 42/8, 29-44, 22 January 1786.
61 Nepean to Treasury, 10 June 1786, T. 1/632.
62 *Nautilus* log ADM. 51/627; and Mackay, *op. cit.*, p. 130.
63 Thompson Journal, ADM. 55/92, 26.
64 Frost, *op. cit.*, p. 120.
65 I.R. Christie, 'The Cabinet in the Reign of George III, to 1790', *Myth and Reality*, p. 70. H.O. 35/1, 18 August 1786. H.O. 35/7, 18 August 1786.

5 THE BOTANY BAY DECISION 1786–7

1   On the ministry's narrow conception of the function of the colony see David Mackay, 'Far-Flung Empire: a Neglected Imperial Outpost at Botany Bay', *The Journal of Imperial and Commonwealth History*, vol. IX, no. 2, January 1981, pp. 125–45.
2   J.C. Beaglehole (ed.), *The Journals of Captain Cook on His Voyages of Discovery*, vol. 1, pp. 310–12. J.C. Beaglehole (ed.), *The Endeavour Journal of Joseph Banks*, vol. 2, pp. 53–6.
3   H.O. 35/1, 18 August 1786.
4   Phillip to Sydney, 11 April 1787, C.O. 201/2, 126–31.
5   See Phillip's Instructions, C.O. 202/5, 28–38, 25 April 1787.
6   Sydney to Lords of Treasury, 31 October 1788, H.O. 35/9.
7   Nepean to Steele, 2 December 1788, *ibid*.
8   Richards to Keeper of Brecon Jail, 5 February 1789, H.O. 42/4, 132–3.
9   H.O. 35/1, 18 August 1786.
10 Sydney to Lords of Adm., 31 August 1786, ADM. 1/4152.
11 On the ships see, P.G. King, *The Journal of Philip Gidley King, Lieutenant R.N., 1787–1790*, p. 5. ADM. 2/262, 468, 12 October 1786; 488, 27 October 1786. Nepean notes, n.d., 1786, H.O. 42/7, 24. Phillip's Instructions, C.O. 202/5, 28–38. Phillip's notes, 11 April 1787, C.O. 201/2, 128.
12 Ross to Nepean, 24 April 1787, C.O. 201/3, 317.
13 *H.R.N.S.W.* vol. 1, pt. 2, pp. 33, 40.
14 Sydney to Lords of Admiralty, 31 August 1786, ADM. 1/4152.
15 D. Collins to G. Collins, 1 January 1787, M.L. Collins Papers FM4/1636.
16 Phillip to Sydney, 12 March 1787, C.O. 201/2, 120–1.
17 Phillip's notes, 11 April 1787, C.O. 201/2, 128-31.

18   Phillip to Sydney, 5 June 1787, C.O. 201/2, 160.
19   R.G. Albion, *Forests and Sea Power*; D.B. Horn, *Great Britain and Europe in the Eighteenth Century*, pp. 202–3, 213–14.
20   R. Davis, *The Rise of the English Shipping Industry*, pp. 175–6, 223–4.
21   B.T. 5/2, 14, 27 July 1783.
22   *Ibid.*, 134, 5 May 1785.
23   Duncan to Banks, 31 December 1783, Kew B.C. 1, 155.
24   Morton to Banks, 13 April 1785, ADD. MSS 33978, 9.
25   B.T. 5/4, 33, 38–42, 7–28 November 1786.
26   B.T. 5/4, 43, 28 November 1786.
27   B.T. 3/1, 165, 29 November 1786.
28   B.T. 5/5, 21–3, 12 February 1788.
29   B.T. 5/12, 106–112, 19 December 1800.
30   H.O. 42/11, 320–1, 24 August 1790. B.T. 5/6, same date.
31   *Ibid.*, J. Goodhall to Banks, 22 December 1800, Kew B.C. 2, 241.
32   B.T. 5/5, 184, 28 June 1789. ADD. MSS 38310, 38, 224, 6 August and 17 November 1789.
33   Bolton, 'The hollow conqueror: flax and the foundation of Australia', *Australian Economic History Review*, vol. 8, 1968, pp. 4–5, 10–11. Brook Watson to Board of Trade, 13 October 1789, B.T. 5/5, 192. *H.R.N.S.W.* vol. 1, pt. 2, p. 471, 4 March 1791.
34   References to flax in despatches are considered further in Chapter 8.
35   Phillip to Nepean, December 1786, H.O. 42/10, 302. Same to same, 2 September 1787, *H.R.N.S.W.* vol. 1, pt 2, p. 113.
36   D.L. Mackay, Ph.D thesis, *op. cit.* D.L. Mackay, 'A Presiding Genius of Exploration: Banks, Cook and Empire, 1767–1805', in R. Fisher and H. Johnson (eds), *Captain Cook and His Times*, pp. 21–39.
37   Atkinson, *op. cit.*
38   Phillip's Instructions, 25 April 1787, C.O. 202/5, 28-38.
39   Phillip to Nepean, 1 March 1787, C.O. 201/2, 114–5.
40   On the equipping of the first fleet see David Mackay, 'Far-Flung Empire: a Neglected Imperial Outpost at Botany Bay', *op. cit.*
41   Frost, *op. cit.*, p. 137.
42   ADM. 2/262, 469, 12 October 1786.
43   W. Bayly to Banks, 8 August 1786, Kew B.C. I, 237. Frost, *op. cit.*, p. 138. Brook Watson to Nepean, 2 November 1786, H.O. 42/10, 393. Phillip to Sydney, 9 July 1788, C.O. 201/3, 45–50.
44   Frost, *op. cit.*, p. 138. J. Cobley, *The Crimes of the First Fleet Convicts*. Phillip to Sydney, 16 November 1788, C.O. 201/3, 147-9. On Morley, *H.R.N.S.W.* vol. 1, pt 2, p. 481.
45   C.N. Parkinson, *Trade in the Eastern Seas, 1793–1813*, pp. 331-3.
46   On the Indian experiments see, J. Sinclair to Banks, 2 May 1799, Kew. B.C. 2, 218. G. Sinclair to Banks, 3 April 1798, N.L.S., Melville Papers, 1064, 125–6. Lady Spencer to Banks, 5 October 1800, ADD. MSS 33980, 249-50. Hugh Inglis to Banks, 6 January 1801, *ibid.*, 260. B.T. 1/17, 292, 29 April 1799. B.T. 5/12, 87, 89–94, 94–6, 98–110, 113–6, 129–136, 147–9, 209, December 1800 to March 1801.
47   Cobley, *op. cit.*

48 Douglas Hay, 'Property, Authority and the Criminal Law', in Hay, Linebaugh and Thompson (eds), *Albion's Fatal Tree*, pp. 42–6.
49 Phillip to Sydney, 9 July 1788, C.O. 201/3, 45–50.
50 Richmond to Grenville, 2 October 1789, H.O. 42/15, 264. H.O. 43/2, 20 February 1791.
51 Le Mesurier to Nepean, 27 November 1786, H.O. 42/10, 414.
52 *H.R.N.S.W.* vol. 1, pt 2, p. 46, 11 January 1787.
53 Phillip to Sydney, 3 December 1786, H.O. 42/10, 303. Solicitor General to Nepean, 25 March 1787, H.O. 48/1b.
54 Nepean to Sydney, 9 November 1786, M.L., A.N. 53/1. Also in N.L. MS 3568.
55 Phillip to Nepean, 4 January 1787, C.O. 201/2, 103–5.
56 Phillip's Instructions, 25 April 1787, C.O. 202/5, 28–38.
57 Middleton to Nepean, 11 December 1786, C.O. 201/2, 51–2.
58 Phillip to Nepean, 4 January, 11 January, 28 February and 18 March 1787, C.O. 201/2, 103–5, 112, 122–3.

6   STRATEGY, COMMERCE AND THE ROUTE TO INDIA

1   A. Frost, *Convicts and Empire*, pp. xii, xiv.
2   H. Furber, *John Company at Work*, p. 69.
3   Frost, *op. cit.*, pp. 87, 121.
4   H.L. Hoskins, *British Routes to India*, p. 83.
5   On St Helena see D.L. Mackay, 'British Interest in the Southern Oceans 1783–1801', *New Zealand Journal of History*, vol. 3, no. 2, 1969, p. 5.
6   V.T. Harlow, *op. cit.*, vol. 1, ch. 4. L.C.F. Turner, 'The Cape of Good Hope in Anglo-French Rivalry', *Historical Studies. Australia and New Zealand*, vol. XI, no. 46, April 1966, pp. 166–85.
7   Johnstone to Lords of Adm., 21 November 1781, H.O. 28/2, 81.
8   Hillsborough to Chairman of the East India Company, January 1782, C.O. 77/25.
9   J. Ehrman, *The Younger Pitt*, pp. 520, 532.
10 *Ibid.*, p. 425.
11 Report of the Beauchamp Committee, 21 June 1785, H.O. 42/6, 457.
12 On the whaling industry in this period, see V.T. Harlow, *op. cit.*, vol. 2, ch. 5. D.L. Mackay, 'British Interest in the Southern Oceans, 1783–1801', *op. cit.*
13 Memorial of Messrs Enderby, St. Barbe and Champion, January 1786, B.T. 6/93. B.T. 5/3, 55–6, 199, 4 February and 26 May 1786. *26 Geo. III, cap 50.*
14 J. Leard to Hawkesbury, 16 July 1788, B.T. 6/95. P.R.O. Chatham Papers 30/8/151, 1–4.
15 Enderby to Banks, 26 August 1788, Kew B.C. 1, 319.
16 Affidavit of Captain Middleton, 25 September 1789, B.T. 6/95.
17 Whalers' Memorial to Leeds, 16 October 1789, B.T. 6/95. B.T. 5/5, 195–6, 26 October 1789.
18 Grenville Memorandum, 17 June 1789, C.O. 77/25.

19   Blankett to Nepean, 4 June 1789, H.O. 42/14, 172. Banks to Nepean, 27 August 1789, H.O. 28/6, 314.
20   Grenville to Lords of Adm., 3 October 1789, ADM. 1/4154, 43. H.O. 28/6, 304–5.
21   ADM. 3/106, 48, 6 October 1789. Menzies to Banks, 8 October 1789, Kew B.C. 1, 362.
22   ADM. 106/2631, 9 and 21 December 1789.
23   ADM. 3/106, 96, 7 December 1789. H.O. 28/6, 382, 7 December 1789.
24   ADM. 3/106, 96, 19 January 1790. ADM. 2/265, 332, same date. ADM. 106/2632, same date.
25   Enderby to Nepean, 18 August 1790, H.O. 42/16. ADM. 3/107, 7 May 1790.
26   ADM 106/2635, 16 November 1790, 11–18 December 1790.
27   A. Menzies, 'Journal of Vancouver's Voyage', ADD. MSS 32641, 1. Roberts to Stephens, 24 December 1790, 23 June 1791, ADM. 1/2395.
28   Ehrman, *op. cit.*, p. 564.
29   Lucas & Co. to Hawkesbury, 23 November 1790, B.T. 6/95.
30   Teast to Board of Trade, 8 January 1791, B.T. 6/95.
31   Grenville to Lords of Adm., 11 February 1791, ADM. 1/4156, 14. H.O. 28/8, 17–24.
32   Frost, *op. cit.*, p. 116.

7   INDIA AND THE EASTERN SEAS

1   Ships *armé en flûte* were former warships converted to merchantmen by the removal of their lower deck guns.
2   This scenario is described in Frost, *op. cit.*, pp. 86, 97–116.
3   S.P. Sen, *The French in India*, p. 537.
4   E. Ingram, *Commitment to Empire: Prophecies of the Great Game in Asia,1797–1800*, chs VI and X.
5   Sen, *op. cit.*, p. 568. C.N. Parkinson, *War in the Eastern Seas, 1793–1815*, p. 276.
6   H.O. 28/60, 126–132, 28 April 1783, Plans for the Disposition of Forces in the East Indies.
7   Admiral Hughes to Stephens, 20 November 1784, ADM. 1/16E, 235-7.
8   Frost, *op. cit.*, p. 95.
9   H. Furber, *John Company at Work*, p. 71.
10   L. Dermigny, *La Chine et L'Occident*, vol. 3, p. 1091; (. . . that the intention of the English is to accustom Europe to expeditions equally and more numerous than that of this year and that . . . on the occasion of a future conflict the same number of vessels similarly sent from Europe will certainly be used . . . for expeditions of a different kind. Forty ships of the power of those of the Company, and deployed to transport the numerous troops which they have on the Coast of Coromandel, into all the Dutch possessions for example, would soon render them mistresses of it all . . . .)

11 E. K. Chatterton, *The Old East Indiamen*, pp. 162-4. Dermigny, *op. cit.*, vol. 1, pp. 212-3. R. Davis, *The Rise of the English Shipping Industry in the Seventeenth and Eighteenth Centuries*, p. 73.
12 Chatterton, *op. cit.*, p. 167.
13 Chatterton, *op. cit.*, p. 274. C.N. Parkinson, *Trade in the Eastern Seas, 1793-1815*, p. 150.
14 Parkinson, *op. cit.*, p. 132.
15 C.N. Parkinson, *War in the Eastern Seas, 1793-1815*, pp.221-31.
16 H.O. 28/60, 126-132, 28 April 1783.
17 Cornwallis to Grenville, 11 November 1789, ADM. 1/167, 31.
18 H.T. Fry, *Alexander Dalrymple and the Expansion of British Trade*, p. 151.
19 Furber, *op. cit.*, p. 6.
20 Dalrymple to Mulgrave, 30 April 1787, N.L. Dalrymple MS 43/6. V.T. Harlow, *op. cit.*, vol. 2, p. 362.
21 Dundas to Cornwallis, 20 July 1787, N.L.S. Melville Papers, 3387, 11-12. Same to same, *ibid.*, 68. P.R.O. Cornwallis Papers 30/11/112, 1-8, 20 July 1787.
22 Harlow, *op. cit.*, pp. 348-53.
23 Sen, *op. cit.*, p. 430.
24 Furber, *op. cit.*, pp. 72-3. Sen, *op. cit.*, p. 400.
25 Furber, *op. cit.*, p. 74.
26 Sydney to Lords of Adm., 25 October 1788, H.O. 28/6, 118. Stephens to Nepean, 23 January 1789, *ibid.*, 166.
27 ADM. 1/167, 50, 19 September 1789.
28 Dundas Memorandum, October 1787, N.L.S. Melville papers 1068, 20-37.

8 NEW SOUTH WALES ESTABLISHED

1 Phillip to Sydney, 5 June 1787, C.O. 201/2, 160.
2 Sir George Young's plan, C.O. 201/2, 55-6.
3 Matra to North, 23 August 1783, C.O. 201/1, 57-61.
4 An example is in A. Bowes Smith, *The Journal of Arthur Bowes Smith, Surgeon, the Lady Penryn*, 1787-9, p. 57.
5 Captain John Campbell to Baron Ducie, 12 July 1788, M.L., Campbell letters A.C. 145, p. 10.
6 B. Fitzpatrick, *British Imperialism and Australia*, pp. 88-91.
7 Phillip to Nepean, 9 and 12 July 1788, C.O. 201/32, 44, 62.
8 C.O. 201/8, 58, 31 May 1793. C.O. 201/11, 37, 29 April 1794.
9 This process is described in B.H. Fletcher, *Landed Enterprise and Penal Society*, chs IV and V.
10 Hunter to Portland, 28 April and 20 August 1796, C.O. 201/13, 11-15, 62.
11 Portland to Hunter, 3 December 1798, 5 November 1799, C.O. 201/14, 314-18, 290-301.
12 See above, chapter 4.
13 Grenville to Phillip, 20 June 1789, C.O. 201/3, 151-2. Frost, *op. cit.*, pp. 78, 84.

14   Phillip's Instructions, 25 April 1787, C.O. 202/5, 28–38.
15   Phillip memorandum, C.O. 201/2, 90–3. Also David Mackay, 'Far-
      Flung Empire', p. 142.
16   Phillip to Sydney, 15 May 1788, C.O. 201/3, 5–24. Phillip to
      Nepean, 5 July 1788, *ibid.*, pp. 41–2. *H.R.N.S.W.* vol. 1, pt. 2, Ap-
      pendix B.
17   Phillip to Nepean, 16 November 1788, C.O. 201/3, 155. Phillip to
      Sydney, 12 February 1790, C.O. 201/5, 15–16. *H.R.N.S.W.*, vol. 1,
      pt. 2. pp. 428, 434.
18   King to Banks, 25 November 1794, M.L. Banks MSS A81, 273–6.
19   Phillip's Instructions, 25 April 1787, C.O. 202/5, 28–38.
20   H.O. 42/7, 24, 1786. C.O. 201/1, 43, 28 November 1786. Phillip
      to Sydney, 11 April 1790, C.O. 201/5, 58.
21   Grenville to Phillip, 14 February 1791, C.O. 201/5, 62–3.
22   Frost, *op. cit.*, pp. 154–7.
23   D.L. Mackay, Ph.D. thesis, *op. cit.*, chs 7 and 8.
24   See 'Heads of Instructions', H.O. 42/16, 10. ADM. 3/107, 48, 25
      February 1790. H.O. 28/61, 259–261, March 1790. C.O. 201/5,
      50, March 1790. Grenville to Cornwallis, 31 March 1790, H.O. 28/
      61, 253–5. Instructions to commander of frigate, 31 March 1790,
      H.O. 28/61, 273.
25   These details on strategy are taken from C.N. Parkinson, *War in the
      Eastern Seas*, 1793–1815. L. Dermigny, *La Chine et L'Occident*, vol. 3,
      ch. 2. E. Ingram, *Commitment to Empire*, chs III, V and VII.
26   Grenville to Phillip, 19 February 1791, C.O. 201/5, 62–771.
27   Phillip to Dundas, 2 October 1792, C.O. 201/7, 52.
28   Instructions to Phillip, C.O. 202/5, 28–38.

9   CONCLUSION

1   V.T. Harlow, *The Founding of the Second British Empire, 1763–1793*,
     vol. I, ch. 3.

BIBLIOGRAPHY

MANUSCRIPT SOURCES

BRITISH ISLES

A Public Record Office

i Admiralty Papers

Captains' Letters,	ADM. 1.
Letters from Secretary of State,	ADM. 1.
Orders and Instructions,	ADM. 2.
Lords' Letters,	ADM. 2.
Secretary's Letters,	ADM. 2.
Admiralty Board Minutes,	ADM. 3.
Logs and Journals,	ADM. 51, 55.
Navy Board,	ADM. 106.

ii Board of Trade Papers

In-letters,	B.T. 1.
Out-letters,	B.T. 3.
Minutes,	B.T. 5.
Miscellaneous, whale fisheries,	B.T. 6/93, 95.
Miscellaneous, hemp and flax,	B.T. 6/97.

iii Colonial Office

East Indies,	C.O. 77.
New South Wales,	C.O. 201, 202.
Vancouver's voyage,	C.O. 5/187.

iv Home Office

Beauchamp Committee minutes,	H.O. 7/1.
Admiralty correspondence,	H.O. 28.
Admiralty entry book,	H.O. 29.
Foreign Office correspondence,	H.O. 32.
Treasury correspondence,	H.O. 35.
Domestic, George III,	H.O. 42.
Secretary, out-letters,	H.O. 43.

Law Officers' reports,	H.O. 49.
Scotland, in-letters,	H.O. 102.
Scotland, out-letters,	H.O. 103.
vi Treasury Papers	
Correspondence,	T. 1
v Private Collections	
Chatham Papers,	P.R.O. 30/8.
Cornwallis Papers,	P.R.O. 30/11

B British Library

Banks Papers,	Add. MSS 8094-7, 33272, 22977-22982.
Fox Papers,	Add. MSS 47568.
Liverpool Papers,	Add. MSS 38310.
Archibald Menzies Journal,	Add. MSS 32641.

C British Museum (Natural History)

Dawson Turner Copies (D.T.C.) of the correspondence of Sir Joseph Banks, vols 1-20.

D Royal Botanic Gardens, Kew

Correspondence of Sir Joseph Banks in the Herbarium Libary, Kew B.C.

E India Office Library

General Correspondence,	E.
Board of Control Letter Book,	F.
Home Miscellaneous Series.	

F National Library of Scotland

Melville Papers.

G Scottish Record Office

Melville Castle Muniments,	G.D. 51.

AUSTRALIA

A National Library of Australia, Canberra

Dalrymple Letters,	MS 43.
Nepean Letters,	MS 3568.
Petherick Collection,	MS 760.

B Mitchell Library, State Library of New South Wales

Banks Letters,	A 78, FM 4/4365.
Campbell Letters,	AC 145.

Collins Letters,   FM 4/1630.
King Papers, Letter Book,   C 187.
Nepean Letters,   AN 53.

PRINTED SOURCES

Fort William—India House Correspondence, XIII, XXII, ed. P.C. Gupta,
   Indian National Archives, New Delhi, 1959
Historical Manuscript Commission (*H.M.C.*), Report on the Correspond-
   ence of J. B. Fortescue, preserved at Dropmore, 30, I–II.
Historical Records of Australia (*H.R.A.*), Library of the Commonwealth
   Parliament, Ist Series.
Historical Records of New South Wales (*H.R.N.S.W.*), I-IV, Sydney,
   1892–1901, eds A. Britton and F.M. Bladen.
The Archives of British Honduras, I, London, 1931, ed. J.A. Burdon.
The Correspondence of George the Third, London, 1928, ed. Sir John
   Fortescue.
The Later Correspondence of George III, Cambridge, 1962, ed. A. Aspin-
   all.

SECONDARY SOURCES

Aspinall, A. *Cornwallis in Bengal*, Manchester University Press, Manchester,
   1931.
Abbott, G.J. and Nairn, N.B. *Economic Growth of Australia 1788–1821*, Mel-
   bourne University Press, Carlton, 1969.
Anderson, B. *Surveyor of the Sea. The Life and Voyages of Captain George Van-
   couver*, Toronto University Press, Toronto, 1960.
Anderson, M.S. *Britain's Discovery of Russia, 1553–1815*, Mathew Smith,
   London, 1958.
Ashton, T.S. *An Economic History of England. The 18th Century*, Methuen,
   London, 1966.
Atkinson, A. 'Whigs and Tories and Botany Bay', *Journal of the Royal Aus-
   tralian Historical Society*, vol. 61, March 1975, pp. 288–310.
—— 'Botany Bay: a counter riposte', *Australian Economic History Review*,
   vol. 17, 1977, pp. 78–82.
Baugh, D.A. *British Naval Administration in the Age of Walpole*, Princeton
   University Press, Princeton, 1965.
Beaglehole, J.C. (ed.). *The Journals of Captain Cook on His Voyages of Discovery*,
   3 vols, Cambridge University Press, for the Hakluyt Society, Cambridge,
   1955–74.
—— *The Endeavour Journal of Joseph Banks*, 2 vols, Public Library of N.S.W.
   in association with Angus and Robertson, Sydney, 1962.
Beattie, J.M. 'The Pattern of Crime in England 1660–1800', *Past & Present*,
   vol. 62, February 1974, pp. 46–95.

Blainey, G. *The Tyranny of Distance*, Sun Books, Melbourne, 1966.
—— 'A Reply: "I came, I Shaw . . ." ', *Historical Studies*, vol. 13, 1968, pp. 204–6.
—— *A Land Half Won*, Macmillan, Adelaide, 1980.
Blaug, M. 'The Myth of the Old Poor Law and the Making of the New', *Journal of Economic History*, vol. XXIII, 1963, pp. 151–84.
Bolton, G.C. 'The Hollow Conqueror: Flax and the Foundation of Australia', *Australian Economic History Review*, vol. 9, 1968, pp. 3–16.
—— 'Broken Reeds and Smoking Flax', *Australian Economic History Review*, vol. 9, 1969, pp. 64–70.
Branch-Johnson, W. *The English Prison Hulks*, Christopher Johnson, London, 1957.
Brewer, J. and Styles, J. (eds). *An Ungovernable People. The English and their Law in the Seventeenth and Eighteenth Centuries*, Hutchinson, London, 1980.
Bowes-Smith, A. *The Journal of Arthur Bowes-Smith, Surgeon, in the Lady Penryn, 1787–9*, Trustees of the Public Library of N.S.W. Sydney, 1979.
Burney, J. *A Chronological History of the Discoveries in the South Sea or Pacific Ocean*, 5 vols, L. Hansard, London, 1803–17.
Chatterton, E.K. *The Old East Indiamen*, Rich and Cowan, London, 1933.
Christie, I.R. *Wars and Revolutions, Britain 1760–1815*, Edward Arnold, London, 1982.
—— *Myth and Reality in Late Eighteenth Century British Politics*, Macmillan, London, 1970.
Clark, C.M.H. *A History of Australia*, vol. 1, Melbourne University Press, Carlton, 1962.
Cobley, J. *The Crimes of the First Fleet Convicts*, Angus and Robertson, Sydney, 1970.
Cockburn, J.S. (ed.) *Crime in England 1550–1800*, Methuen, London, 1977.
Collins, D. *An Account of the English Colony in New South Wales*, Cadell, London, 1798.
Dallas, K.M. *Trading Posts or Penal Colonies. Cook's Route to Pacific Trade*, C.L. Richmond and Sons, Hobart, 1969.
Dalrymple, A. *An Account of the Discoveries Made in the Pacific Ocean Previous to 1764*, published by the author, London, 1967.
—— *An Historical Collection of Voyages and Discoveries in the South Pacific Ocean*, published by the author, London, 1770–1.
—— *A Collection of Voyages Chiefly in the Southern Atlantick Ocean*, published by the author, London, 1775.
Davies K.G. *The Royal Africa Company*, Longmans, London, 1957.
Davis, R. *The Rise of the English Shipping Industry in the Seventeenth and Eighteenth Centuries*, Macmillan, London, 1962.
Dawson, W. (ed.). *The Banks Letters*, Trustees of the British Museum, London, 1958.
De, B. 'Henry Dundas and the Government of India, 1773-1801', unpublished Oxford D.Phil., 1961.
Dermigny, L. *La Chine et L'Occident. Le Commerce a Canton au XVIIIe Siècle, 1719–1833*, 3 vols, S.E.V.P.E.N., Paris, 1964.
Dow, G. *Samuel Terry, the Botany Bay Rothschild*, Sydney University Press, Sydney, 1974.
Dunmore, J. *French Explorers in the Pacific*, vol. 1, Oxford University Press, Oxford, 1965.
Easty, J. *Memorandum of the Transactions of a Voyage from England to Botany*

Bay 1787–1793, Trustees of the Public Library of N.S.W. with Angus and Robertson, Sydney, 1965.

Ehrman, J. *The Younger Pitt*, Constable, London, 1969.

Evans, L. and Nicholls, P. *Convicts and Colonial Society*, 1788–1853, Cassell, Stanmore, 1976.

Finberg, H.P.R. (ed.). *Gloucestershire Studies*, Leicester University Press, 1953.

Fisher, R. and Johnson, H. (eds). *Captain Cook and His Times*, Croom Helm, London, 1980.

Fitzpatrick, B. *British Imperialism and Australia: An Economic History of Australasia*, Allen and Unwin, London, 1939.

Fletcher, B.H. *Landed Enterprise and Penal Society. A History of Farming and Grazing in New South Wales before 1821*, Sydney University Press, Sydney, 1978.

Frost, A. *Convicts and Empire. A Naval Question*, Oxford University Press, Melbourne, 1980.

—— 'The Choice of Botany Bay. The scheme to supply the East Indies with naval stores', *Australian Economic History Review*, vol. 15, 1975, pp. 1–20.

—— 'The East India Company and the Choice of Botany Bay', *Historical Studies*, vol. 16, 1975, pp. 606–12.

—— 'Botany Bay: A Further Commment', *Australian Economic History Review*, vol. 17, 1977, pp. 64–77.

Fry, H.T. *Alexander Dalrymple and the Expansion of British Trade*, Frank Cass, London, 1970.

—— 'Early British Interest in the Chagos Archipelago and Maldive Islands', *Mariners' Mirror*, vol. LIII, 1967, pp. 343–56.

—— ' "Cathay and the Way Thither". The Background to Botany Bay', *Historical Studies*, vol. 14, 1969–71, pp. 497–510.

Furber, H. *John Company at Work*, Harvard University Press, Cambridge, Mass., 1948.

—— *Rival Empires of Trade in the Orient 1600–1800*, Oxford University Press, Minn., 1974.

Gailey, H.A. *A History of the Gambia*, Routledge and Kegan Paul, London, 1964.

Gill, C. *Merchants and Mariners of the Eighteenth Century*, Greenwood, Westport, Conn., 1971.

Gillen, M. 'The Botany Bay Decision, 1786: convicts not empire', *English Historical Review*, vol. XCVII, no. 385, October 1982, pp. 740-66.

Gray, J.M. *History of the Gambia*, Frank Cass, London, 1966.

Greenwood, G. *Australia. A Social and Political History*, Angus and Robertson, Sydney, 1955.

Hainsworth, D.R. *Builders and Adventurers. The Traders and the Emergence of the Colony*, Cassell, Melbourne, 1968.

—— *The Sydney Traders. Simeon Lord and his Contemporaries*, Cassell, Sydney, 1974.

Hallett, R. *The Penetration of Africa*, Routledge and Kegan Paul, London, 1965.

Hallward, N.L. *William Bolts*, Cambridge University Press, Cambridge, 1920.

Harlow, V.T. *The Founding of the Second British Empire, 1763–1793*, 2 vols, Longmans, London, 1964.

—— and Madden, F. *British Colonial Developments 1774–1834*, Oxford University Press, Oxford, 1953.

Hay, D. 'War, Dearth and Theft in the Eighteenth Century', *Past & Present*, vol. 95, May 1982, pp. 117-60.

Hay, D., Linebaugh, P. and Thompson, E.P. *Albion's Fatal Tree. Crime and Society in Eighteenth Century England*, Allen Lane, London, 1975.

Hirst, J.B. *Convict Society and its Enemies. A History of Early New South Wales*, Allen and Unwin, Sydney, 1983.

Horn, D.B. *Great Britain and Europe in the Eighteenth Century*, Oxford University Press, Oxford, 1967.

Hoskins, H.L. *British Routes to India*, Frank Cass, London, 1966, reprint.

Howard, J. *The State of the Prisons*, Everyman, London, 1929.

Hyam, R. and Martin, G. *Reappraisals in British Imperial History*, Macmillan, London, 1975.

Ignatieff, M. *A Just Measure of Pain. The Penitentiary in the Industrial Revolution 1750-1850*, Macmillan, London, 1978.

Ingram, E. *Commitment to Empire: Prophecies of the Great Game in Asia, 1797-1800*, Oxford University Press, Oxford, 1981.

King, P.G. *The Journal of Philip Gidley King, Lieutenant R.N.*, Trustees of the Public Library of N.S.W., Sydney, 1980.

Linge, G.J.R. *Industrial Awakening. A Geography of Australian Manufacturing 1788-1890*, Australian National University Press, Canberra, 1979.

Love, H.D. *Vestiges of Old Madras*, 4 vols, Murray, London, 1913.

Mackay, D.L. 'British Interest in the Southern Oceans, 1782-1794', *New Zealand Journal of History*, vol. 3, no. 2, October 1869, pp. 124-42.

—— 'Direction and Purpose in British Imperial Policy, 1783-1801', *The Historical Journal*, vol. XVII, no. 3, 1974, pp. 487-501.

—— 'Far-Flung Empire: A Neglected Imperial Outpost at Botany Bay, 1788-1801', *Journal of Imperial and Commonwealth History*, vol. IX, no. 2, January 1981, pp. 125-45.

—— 'Exploration and the Economic Development of Empire, 1782-1798', University of London, unpublished Ph.D. thesis, 1970.

Mahan, A.T. *The Influence of Sea Power upon History 1660-1783*, Methuen, London, 1965.

Markham, C.R. *Major James Rennell and the Rise of Modern English Geography*, Macmillan, London, 1895.

Martin, E.C. *The British West Africa Settlements 1750-1821*, Longmans, London, 1927.

Martin, G. 'A London Newspaper on the Founding of Botany Bay, August 1786-May 1787', *Journal of the Royal Australian Historical Society*, vol. 61, pt 2, 1975, pp. 73-90.

—— (ed.). *The Founding of Australia*, Hale and Iremonger, Sydney, 1978.

Martin-Allanic, J.E. *Bougainville Navigateur et les Descouvertes de son Temps*, 2 vols, Presse Universitaire de France, Paris, 1964.

Mitchell, B.R. *Abstract of British Historical Statistics*, Cambridge University Press, Cambridge, 1963.

Money, J. *Experience and Identity. Birmingham and the West Midlands, 1760-1800*, Manchester University Press, Manchester, 1977.

Namier, Sir L. and Brooke, J. *The History of Parliament. The House of Commons 1754-1790*, 3 vols, History of Parliament Trust, London, 1964.

Nelson, R.R. *The Home Office 1782-1801*, Duke University Press, Durham, North Carolina, 1969.

Norris, J.M. 'The Policy of the British Cabinet in the Nootka Crisis', *English Historical Review*, vol. LXX, October 1955, pp. 562-80.

O'Brien, E. *The Foundation of Australia*, Angus and Robertson, Sydney, 1937.

Parkinson, C.N. *Trade in the Eastern Seas 1793–1813*, Cambridge University Press, Cambridge, 1937.

—— *War in the Eastern Seas 1793–1813*, Cambridge University Press, Cambridge, 1954.

Parry, J.H. *Trade and Dominion. The European Overseas Empires in the Eighteenth Century*, Weidenfeld and Nicolson, London, 1971.

Philips, C.H. *The East India Company 1784–1834*, Manchester University Press, Manchester, 1940.

—— (ed.). *The Correspondence of David Scott*, Camden Society, London, 1951.

Radzinowicz, Sir L. *A History of the English Criminal Law and its Administration*, 4 vols, Stevens, London, 1948–68.

Rainaud, A. *Le Continent Austral*, A. Colin et Cie. Paris, 1890.

Reid, L. *Charles James Fox*, Longmans, London, 1969.

Richmond, Sir H. *The Navy in India 1763–1783*, Ernest Benn, London, 1931.

Robson, L.L. *The Convict Settlers of Australia*, Melbourne University Press, Carlton, 1965.

Roe, M. 'Australia's Place in the "Swing to the East" 1788–1810', *Historical Studies*, vol. 8, 1958, pp. 202–13.

Sen, S.P. *The French in India*, Mukhopadyay, Calcutta, 1958.

Shaw, A.G.L. *Convicts and the Colonies*, Faber, London, 1967.

—— 'The Hollow Conqueror and the Tyranny of Distance', *Historical Studies*, vol. 13, 1968, pp. 195–203.

Sharp, A. *The Discovery of Australia*, Oxford University Press, Oxford, 1963.

Spray, W.A. 'British Surveys in the Chagos Archipelago and attempts to form a settlement at Diego Garcia in the late Eighteenth Century', *Mariners' Mirror*, vol. 56, no. 1, January 1970, pp. 59–76.

Steven, M. *Merchant Campbell, 1769–1846. A Study in Colonial Trade*, Oxford University Press, Melbourne, 1965.

—— *Trade, Tactics and Territory. Britain in the Pacific, 1783-1823*, Melbourne University Press, Melbourne, 1983.

Turner, L.C.F. 'The Cape of Good Hope and Anglo-French Rivalry 1778-1796', *Historical Studies*, vol. 12, 1966, pp. 166-85.

Ward, J.M. *British Policy in the South Pacific 1786-1893*, Australian Publishing Company, Sydney, 1948.

INDEX

Bligh, Capt. William 99
Board of Control 86
Board of Trade (Privy Council
  Committee on Trade and
  Plantations) 62, 63, 66, 76,
  77, 81
Bolton, G.C. 6
Bombay 35, 73, 87
Boone, Mr 48
Borneo 33
Botany Bay 1, 12, 39, 40, 42,
  45, 49, 64–5, 91
  decision to settle 7, 51, 56
  doubts expressed about 57,
  91
Bowen, John 98
Bradley, Richard 45, 48, 54
breadfruit 26
Britain 5, 7, 75
  and France 71, 80, 82, 86,
  97
  imperial policy 3, 75, 100
  naval strategy 7, 28, 72
  naval strength 80, 81, 84–5,
  88, 89
  and Netherlands 71, 86, 88,
  97
  and Spain 72, 77, 79–80
Broughton, William 99
Bruny D'Entrecasteaux, J.A.
  85
Bunbury Committee *see*
  Committee on Transportation
Burke, Edmund 47

Caffre Coast 34
Calcutta 67, 98
Call, Sir John 6, 25, 37, 47–8
  plans for New South Wales
    31–4
  plans for Norfolk Island 33, 36
  seeks job at Das Voltas Bay
    52
Calonne, Charles-Alexandre 84
Calvert, Anthony 46, 47
Campbell, Duncan 13, 53
  estimates on transportation to
    New South Wales 49, 55
  evidence to Bunbury
    Committee 38–9

evidence to Beauchamp
  Committee 48–50
Campbell, John 91
Canada 38–9, 47, 62
Canton 85
Cape Coast Castle 32, 40, 42
Cape of Good Hope 7, 58, 73,
  78, 83, 96
  attacks on 8, 81, 88, 97
  strategic position 60, 71, 75
Cape Horn 78, 81
Ceylon 71, 73, 88
Chatham, 2nd Earl *see* Pitt,
  John
China 30, 33, 61, 75, 85
Clark, C.M.H. 6
Clerke, Charles 27
Cobley, John 4, 66
Cochin China 86
Coggan, Mr 49
coir 33, 66
Collins, David 60
Colquhuon, Patrick 19
Committee of Merchants Trading
  to Africa 42, 44, 45
Committee on Transportation,
  1779 (Bunbury) 39–40
Committee on Transportation,
  1785 (Beauchamp) 2, 14,
  28, 31, 32, 37, 47–53, 75,
  81
  evidence before 39, 41,
  43–50
Compagnie des Indies Orientales
  see East India Company,
  French
contagion *see* diseases
convicts
  diseases among 17, 68
  escapes 16, 18
  increased numbers 6, 15,
  20, 22–3
  in hulks 13, 18
  labour 18, 69
  occupations 67
  selection for first fleet 67–8
convict colonies
  commercial value 32
  in Africa 39, 40, 44–9
  passim, 93
  in America 10, 13, 22, 38–41, 58